Forty Delicious Years

Top left: Murni, Tooth-filing, Ubud, 1992; right: Murni's aunt, Murni sitting, her mother to her right, the rest are neighbours, *Kuningan* Day, Denpasar, 1954.

Middle: Murni, her grandmother, a neighbour and Murni's aunt, Ubud, 1992; right above: Murni and her mother, Ubud, 1992; right below: Murni, Sanur, circa 1971.

Bottom: Murni, Sanur, circa 1967; middle and right: Murni, Sanur, circa 1971.

Forty Delicious Years
1974 - 2014

Murni's Warung, Ubud, Bali:
From Toasted Sandwiches to Balinese Smoked Duck

Jonathan Copeland
Rob Goodfellow
Peter O'Neill

Orchid Press

FORTY DELICIOUS YEARS 1974 TO 2014
Murni's Warung, Ubud, Bali:
From Toasted Sandwiches to Balinese Smoked Duck
Compiled by Jonathan Copeland, Rob Goodfellow & Peter O'Neill

ORCHID PRESS
P.O. Box 19,
Yuttitham Post Office,
Bangkok 10907, Thailand
www.orchidbooks.com

Cover image: Ni Wayan Murni, photographed by Jonathan Copeland. Copyright © Jonathan Copeland, 2014.

ISBN: 978-974-524-181-7

The Menu

Foreword

I've been travelling to Bali for over twenty-five years now—a neophyte compared with some of our contributors—but from first landing I knew that it was a place replete with magic and a sort of magnetic power, the kind that would draw me back again and again. Somehow, though, through all of those years and visits, right up until about five years ago, I managed to miss out on one of the island's crown jewels—Ibu Murni.

That changed when I was approached by Jonathan Copeland in 2008 about the possibility of publishing his and Murni's wonderful book, *Secrets of Bali*. Jonathan had put on his 'lawyerly' cloak during the contract discussions and there were times, I confess, when I wondered just how well we would work together. I've long believed that if a project, publishing or otherwise, was not fun, then it was generally not worth undertaking, no matter the prospective rewards…

Murni's Warung, 2014

Once we concluded an agreement though, Jonathan's disguise quickly came off, and to my relief and good fortune, he and Murni turned out to be two of the most graceful, amiable and accommodating authors I have worked with—a relationship that soon evolved into a warm friendship as well.

Jonathan, Rob and Peter originally invited me to contribute to one of the forty 'courses' the reader will enjoy below, a task that I felt I was really not qualified for, in the face of so many who have known Murni for decades—much as I share their feelings and impressions of this remarkable lady.

I'm thus delighted to be able to contribute my own accolades to Murni in the role of publisher of this volume, that I am sure will be enjoyed by all who have met her, and many more who have yet to experience that pleasure.

And last and most importantly, my wife, Lily, and I would like to offer our own personal blessings to Ibu Murni on the wonderful occasion of this anniversary, and to wish her many, many more to come.

Chris Frape
Publisher, Orchid Press,
January 2014

Preface

Murni's Warung, 1979

It is with an enormous sense of disbelief that I am sitting here and writing these words. It is quite incredible to me that I started *Murni's Warung* with a bowl of soup and a sandwich forty years ago. I wasn't a cook and had no knowledge of what Western food was. I had no business plan, no mission statement, and no spreadsheets. I didn't have electricity or a fridge or an electric oven. I didn't have staff or suppliers or a car.

I did have passion and drive and energy. And I had friends and customers and hard work. Luckily *Murni's Warung* grew and prospered and has been able to serve food and drink to thousands of people these forty years. I hope that my guests have enjoyed it. Of course, it was not just me, although it was just me at the very beginning, along with my two cousins. From very early on I was able to employ people, some of whom are still working with me at *Murni's Warung*, and it goes without saying that I am very grateful to all of them for their help, friendship and kindness.

Murni's Warung is probably as famous for its location as

for its food. It is built on a gorge above the River Wos, a river which is sacred to the Balinese. It has been part of my life, going back more than forty years. When I was a very young child of five or six, I played and bathed down there at the river and among the rocks. When I was older, I helped carry rocks up from the river bed to the road for construction use. Later still, after my parents split up, I secretly met my mother below the bridge. I never dreamed that I would be able to buy part of the gorge, live there and go to sleep to the sound of the sacred river crashing over the rocks.

Murni's Warung would be nothing, however, without its guests. It's impossible to know how many have passed through the doors since 1974, but it's hundreds of thousands. Peter Wetzel (1948-2002) was one dear friend, who took the photograph of the *Warung* in 1979. Many come back again and again. Many have become lasting and dear friends. They have come from all corners of the World, and they are still coming and I thank them all.

I am very touched by the recollections of the forty guests for forty years, set out in this book, which I shall treasure for the rest of my life. I hope that you enjoy reading their stories.

Murni
Ubud, Bali
www.murnis.com

About Ibu Murni

Ibu Murni

Murni was born in Penestanan, a few minutes' walk from Ubud. As a very young girl, in the 1950's, she lived in Denpasar, selling breakfast snacks before she went to school.

During the 1960's she was back in Ubud, living with her mother in Ubud market, and learning the trade.

By the early 1970's she owned four shops on Sanur beach and had founded *Murni's Warung*, her famous restaurant, in Campuhan-Ubud, and was on the way to becoming one of the most famous people in Bali.

She built *Murni's Houses*, accommodation for guests, and three shops in Ubud in the 1980's, and began to travel extensively.

Throughout the 1990's she developed and designed *Murni's Villas* in a quiet village in the hills about 15-20 minutes' outside Ubud.

During all this time she was busy collecting and becoming an expert on Asian antiques and textiles and many of them are to be found in *Murni's Warung Shop* beside the restaurant.

In 2007 and 2009 she exhibited part of her collection at the prestigious shows in San Francisco and gave a lecture on Balinese textiles to the Asian Arts Council at the *de Young Museum*.

Secrets of Bali, Fresh Light on the Morning of the World by Jonathan Copeland and Ni Wayan Murni was published in 2010; now in its second print run, it may be purchased in fine bookshops in Bali and around the region. It is also available as an ebook on www.murnis.com.

Murni's Very Personal Guide to Ubud by Ni Wayan Murni and photographs by Jonathan Copeland was published in October 2011 and is available as an ebook on www.murnis. com, Amazon, iBookstore, Barnes & Noble and elsewhere.

From Tattoos to Textiles, Murni's Guide to Asian Textiles, All You Need to Know... And More by Ni Wayan Murni and Jonathan Copeland was published in October 2013 and is available as an ebook on www.murnis.com, Amazon, iBookstore, Barnes & Noble and elsewhere.

Her latest venture, *Tamarind Spa at Murni's Houses*, is intended to bring all these aspects of Balinese art, luxury and culture together in one healing experience.

40 Main Courses

Memories of Murni

Karen Goodman

I lived in Bali for nearly two years in the late 1970's. I was working on a film as part of a college senior thesis. Living in Pengosekan, Penestanan and Sayan, *Murni's Warung* was THE place.

Actually, I believe it was the only place of its kind at that time on the entire island. Here, travellers, adventurers, wanderers, students, researchers and those of us who had extended our stays in Indonesia and just needed to escape to the cool highlands of central Bali, would gather for a cold beer or a mixed juice and a scrumptious meal and always there was lovely and engaging company. Murni, with her effervescent smile and her welcoming staff of lovely young ladies, became our friends and were always part of the lively conversation amongst us.

More than just a place to eat, *Murni's Warung* felt like the best clubhouse in the Universe; a special place for a refreshing drink or a candlelight evening of camaraderie before wandering home through the moonlit rice fields.

Karen Goodman is a Manhattan-based Academy Award winning documentary filmmaker (*Strangers No More, 2010.*) In addition to three other Oscar nominations and a number of Emmy awards, she is the recipient of the Dupont-Columbia Award for Independent Programming (*Buckminster Fuller: Thinking Out Loud, 1996.*) She made her first documentary, *Light of Many Masks (1981)*, in Bali. www. simongoodmanpictures.com.

My Oldest Friend in Bali

Professor Michael Hitchcock

It was on trips to Ubud with my Indonesian sponsor, the late and renowned Professor Dr. I Gusti Ngurah Bagus, that I had my first introduction to Murni's wonderful food. In 1980, Bali's Udayana University had kindly sponsored my research in Bima, on the Indonesian island of Sumbawa, and so it was necessary for me to pop back to Bali from time to time and it was on these occasions that Bapak Bagus would take me with him to Ubud. I eventually ended staying there on many occasions and thus became a regular at *Murni's Warung*. And it really was a *warung* in those days: it was small and welcoming and the menus were always being modified to take account of what ingredients were in season—and so the food was invariably fresh.

Murni was also a fantastic host, providing sparkling conversation and invaluable insights into the culture of Bali and life in Ubud. I also quickly learned that Murni had another side to her and that we both shared a strong interest in the arts and crafts. She could quickly grasp the aesthetic value of whatever she looked at. To my delight, I also found that her range was (and still is) not limited to Indonesian artefacts but extends to nearby countries such as Thailand, Malaysia and Burma. In fact, as I have discovered, Murni has a strong interest in a very wide variety of artistic forms, especially Indonesian textiles. So, it is not just food and a good time that you get at *Murni's Warung*, but a complete sensual experience that embraces all forms of material and visual culture. Murni and I hit it off from the outset and we quickly became good friends; I have just realized in writing this that she is my oldest friend in Bali.

Professor Michael Hitchcock is Dean of the Faculty of Hotel Management and Tourism at Macau University of Science and Technology (formerly the Academic Director and Dean of the IMI University Centre in Lucerne). On completion of his doctorate at the University of Oxford in 1983, he began his professional career teaching in higher education in the UK. Following six years at the University of Hull, he was appointed Professor of Tourism at the University of North London in 1995 and a Centenary Professor the following year. In 2000 he was appointed Director of the International Institute for Culture, Tourism and Development at London Metropolitan University and in 2008 he became Deputy Dean at the University of Chichester. He has written and edited fourteen books, many on Indonesia, as well as many other published outputs. Professor Hitchcock is originally from the UK, but he has lived in Germany, the Netherlands and Indonesia and has taught on British Council funded programmes in Malaysia, Tanzania, Ghana and India.

The Place

Jero Asri Kerthyasa

It was December 1977 and I again found myself in Bali, having resigned from my job, ready to spend three well-deserved months in paradise. Little did I know that I would, in fact, spend the rest of my life here!

My husband and I built our house and a small homestay *Tjetjak Inn* in Campuhan. Life was simple in those days. We had no electricity, no running water, no refrigeration and no telephone. Every day and all day, we ate simple Balinese food. We were young and money was tight. For a Sydney girl swapping city life for village life, it sounds romantic but the truth is that it was hard to turn back the clock and live without modern comforts and conveniences. I yearned for food from home. I couldn't even light the kerosene stove we cooked on!

I vividly remember the joy of going to *Murni's Warung*, especially when the going got tough. It was my haven, my escape. In those days they had a mouthwateringly delicious creation called 'the Upper Elk Valley Burger'. Imagine! And it was heaven! I had found a special place where I would recharge my 'Western batteries'. What joy! When our first child was born, I would take him for a walk and for some reason we always ended up at *Murni's Warung*. I think I had the first stroller in Bali, and I would strap Tjok De in and set off down our dirt path and onto the 'main road' which was little more than a track too. There he would sit contently while I got my 'fix'.

In those days, the seating was at street level and we would sit with an elbow on the windowsill watching the passing parade—ducks, bicycles, women with baskets of vegetables, the very odd car which was usually an old Chevy and then farmers returning from their fields. The old bridge was then the only bridge and traffic was minimal. I remember buying a hand-made book called *Method of Flute Playing*, lovingly handwritten and illustrated by Roda and purchased, accordingly, through the window.

When my parents came to visit, their first port of call was always at *Murni's*. When they were paying I added my favourite Planter's Punch to the order... and always an Upper Elk Valley Burger. While they were visiting, we would often walk over to *Murni's*, torch in hand, for dinner. On the way home we would catch fireflies and fill our pockets with them.

Murni and Pat were always there and their daughter, Morny, and our son, Tjok Gde, were of similar age. It was fun to hang out there. It was 'the hub'. It was where you saw the other expatriates in town and caught up on all the gossip.

Sometimes, cheesecake was on the menu. This could only happen when Murni's friends would bring Philadelphia Cream Cheese from Australia. You had to be quick though; it was very popular and supplies were intermittent. Other favourites were the chocolate chip cookies, the *brem* (rice wine) with ice and lemon, *lumpia* (spring rolls) to die for and the cakes... my goodness the cakes. *Murni's Warung* was THE place in those slower, simpler days.

To this day my mother, now in her late 80s, cannot come to Bali without enjoying at least 'a few meals' at *Murni's*. The walk there is different now. There are no more fireflies (at least until you get well out of town); no torch is needed; the shops are wall-to-wall and the traffic is sometimes frantic. *Murni's* is the Bali she remembers and loved. It's 'her Bali'. It is an institution. It is a favourite and a hive of memories and friendships. It is *Murni's Warung*.

Jero Asri Kerthyasa was born in Singapore, grew up in Sydney and is growing old in Bali. She has lived in Ubud since 1977 and is married to Tjokorda Raka Kerthyasa from *Puri Ubud*. Jero started out with *Tjetjak Inn* in Campuhan, which then grew into *Ibah Hotel*. She now owns and manages *Biku Restaurant* in Seminyak with one of her sons and is busily educating the masses in the joys of High Tea.

Missed the 1970's but I'm early for 2014

Peter Smith

I was born in the 1950's and so, by the 1970's, I really should have been one of the first Australians of my generation to set out on the 'hippy trail' to Bali (and beyond to India and Afghanistan)—and indeed, I had every intention of doing so. Sadly, a decade of illness meant that I did not 'discover Ubud' until good health returned and only then after the passage of nearly thirty years.

As a child growing up in Australia, some good friends were from a Dutch family who had lived in Indonesia and so *gado-gado, saté ayam,* and *nasi goreng* were familiar to me.

My well-travelled contemporaries, however, shook their heads and kindly warned me, 'Bali has changed' and 'it's not like it was in the old days' when *Jalan Kuta* was a dirt track that ended where the coconut groves of Legian began and the only lighting in Ubud was by hurricane lantern or candle.

What I did find in Ubud was the thriving 'capital' of Balinese arts and culture: a vibrant and bustling hamlet of elaborately carved temples and moss-covered Hindu statues, intriguing urban laneways and village walking tracks, markets and stalls, and open-terraced restaurants set on a cool central highlands ridge in a sea of *padi* fields—that change from green to gold with the approaching harvest—and are especially beautiful from the veranda of *Murni's Villas*, where Murni herself hosted me to lunch—a veritable feast of Balinese delicacies, many of which were recipes passed down from her mother.

Ubud also proved to be the ideal base for exploring Besakih (the Mother Temple), Bangli's Pura Kehen, Mount Kintamani and the extraordinary views of Mount Batur and Lake Batur, the Pura Ulun Danu Batur temple with its picturesque multi-tiered *merus*, Gunung Kawi and Yeh Pulu rock-cut carvings, Goa Gajah 'Elephant Cave', the Pura Tirta Empul Holy Spring Temple and the 11th century Gunung Kawi rock-cut monument located near Tampaksiring village.

And of course, all this exploring can give a man a great appetite. Today Ubud is an international food lovers' paradise—every night my friends took me somewhere different—and my high expectations of Balinese food from my childhood meals with my Dutch-Australian friends became even higher.

In 1974 I may have missed the toasted cheese and tomato sandwiches for sale to passers-by on the roadside at *Murni's Warung* near the Old Dutch Bridge—but I'm definitely early for the gastronomic feast of Indonesian food one can experience in Ubud forty years later in 2014.

Peter Smith has enjoyed a long and rich 'catholic' working life involving paying colossal amounts of taxation to the government through careers as diverse as an industrial chemist, commercial radio announcer and rehabilitation counsellor. These days, his overwhelming preoccupation is not with the daily grind, but with the pursuit of happiness.

More than Beauty: Grace and Elegance

Dr. Sally Gray

I visited Bali for the first time in May 1972. In Ubud and Sanur, the atmosphere of the artists and intellectuals who had spent time painting in Bali and learning and writing about Balinese culture, could still be felt. People like Miguel Covarrubias, Colin McPhee, Walter Spies and Donald Friend had left footsteps in which I sensed I was now walking. In dusty, old-style curio shops in seemingly out of the way places like Klungkung and Singaraja, one had a sense of the Muslim and Chinese traders who had moved textiles and spices, silver and precious stones all over the archipelago.

I was a 26-year old Australian who had spent several months following a self-fashioned grand tour of obscure cultural sites all over Italy. I then married in London. Our drive towards discovery matched each other's and we shortly set out to travel back to Australia via Asia. We arrived in Bali after Jakarta and Yogyakarta, having visited Borobudur when it was still a tumbled-down mountain of stones in the jungle. Bali was visually ravishing in a way I had never experienced before. It wasn't just a matter of a beautiful site here and there; it was beautiful everywhere— the buildings, the gestural style and posture of the people, the constant attention to grace and elegance in presentation, in temple and dress and in the ubiquitous presence of ritual— seemingly at every place and in every moment. To an outsider it seemed peaceful.

As two riders on a lone motorbike, we saw hardly any traffic as we moved up and down the east coast. Even Denpasar, where we visited the museum and antique shops and galleries, was relatively quiet. Kuta was deserted; groves of coconut trees were everywhere—right to the sea—and tethered cattle musically grazed through the trees with bells around their necks. We stayed in one of the little bamboo and matting bungalows some villagers had enterprisingly built for the travellers coming through on the 'hippie trail'—from Turkey, Iran, India and Penang—the way through Central Asia to Southeast Asia being still open prior the Iranian revolution in 1979. In Bali then, as now, one met everyone from everywhere. *Barong* and *Kecak* dance performances took place on the sand in the centre of Kuta village, not in a *banjar* building, let alone a hotel. I can't remember where we stayed in Ubud but it was somewhere near rice fields. Everything was near rice fields then. *Murni's Warung* wasn't opened yet and I vaguely remember that we ate at *Tjampuhan Hotel*, although breakfast of tea, bananas and scrambled eggs would have been brought to the front veranda of our little (no fan, no air-conditioning) *losmen* room.

My personal aesthetic was permanently changed by being exposed to Southeast Asian architecture and decorative arts. Euro-centric conceptions of what was beautiful, based on my university study of history and art, were not entirely superseded. But my exposure to Straits Chinese (now Peranakan) architecture and textiles had shaken my earlier conceptions. Certainly it was the Balinese approach to an aesthetic of living, in which art was not separated from life, which I found utterly compelling. With hindsight, I can see that my first and subsequent trips to Bali have had a permanent influence on the way I think about aesthetics, not to mention the fact that I wear *sarongs* to bed, the terrace of my apartment has five frangipani trees on it and incense lighting is a daily ritual.

I first went to *Murni's Warung* in July 1983; it was a romantic holiday in Bali with my husband who was then working in London while I was working in Sydney. *Murni's* restaurant was by then a landmark at the old Tjampuhan Bridge. The people whom I worked closely with in Sydney in the early Eighties were all annual visitors to Bali, spoke Indonesian well and loved *Murni's*. This time we were at different stages of our lives and Bali was now a mass tourism destination, so we stayed in 'real' hotels. It was still gorgeous and *Murni's* retained the aesthetic traditions that people had learned to value about the Bali that could be experienced at Ubud.

Over the years of coming and going in the Eighties and Nineties—like many other Australians—I learned more about the *niskala* and *sekala* of Bali. I came to a profound respect for the human ingenuity embedded in the created Balinese landscape and the complex layers of meaning in the history and practices, which seemed merely beautiful in 1972.

Dr. Sally Gray is a writer, curator and artist who lives and works in Sydney. She is a Visiting Scholar in Cultural History at the College of Fine Arts, University of New South Wales. www.sallygray.com.au. Photograph by Grant Turner.

Bali... Strengthened, not Diminished

Nigel Mason

Made Karyani 'Yanie' (who was born and raised in the then sleepy coconut growing village of Legian) and I married in 1984 and opened *Yanie's Restaurant and Bar* in Legian, Kuta that same year. This was some ten years after the founding of *Murni's Warung* in Ubud. Prior to our marriage, my wife and I had only two places that we could go to keep away from prying eyes and gossip, as a Balinese girl going out with a Westerner in the early 1980's was still frowned upon by the locals. One place was *Tanjung Sari* in Sanur and the other was *Murni's Warung* in Ubud. Most weekends, Yanie and I would travel to Ubud by motorbike and have lunch at *Murni's*. Every time, we finished off our meal with Murni's amazing carrot cake.

In fact, we would usually buy a whole cake to take home with us to enjoy later. *Murni's* was also a favourite place for us to take friends and a few VIP guests, including the actor Jean-Claude Van Damme in 1994 and David Copperfield, the magician, a couple of years later. We have always looked on *Murni's Warung* as a pioneer, like ourselves, and admired the restaurant's uncomplicated but exotic setting—and high quality of service—something that Yanie and I, and now our two adult sons, have emulated over the years with our own businesses. (Recently I discovered that Ibu Murni was in fact 'a regular' at *Yanie's Restaurant* 'in the early days'—so in a way we were growing together.)

In 1989, we built the first White Water Rafting operation in Bali, constructing it to the highest international standards. We wanted literally anyone to be able to get down to the river and raft. It was an instant success. Today our operations stand alone amongst dozens of companies as the island's only 'Five-star' operation, using 21st century design, modern amenities, trained river guides and the best rafting gear and safety equipment in the World. *The Elephant Safari Park* at Taro, near Ubud, was conceived and built over a period of many years, starting in 1997, with only nine elephants. Currently, there are thirty resident pachyderms at the park, with the park now listed as Bali's 'number 1 must see attraction'. Both the *White Water Rafting* and the *Elephant Safari Park* were the first of their kind (not unlike *Murni's Warung*) and were pioneered by *Bali Adventure Tours*. Both businesses set high standards and forced the 'copycat' companies that sprang up to at least try to duplicate what we have done—also something we have in common with *Murni's Warung*.

Since I arrived on the island thirty-two years ago, there have been some very dramatic changes. It's always the negative changes that we hear about, like too many buildings and too much road traffic, but I like to think of the positive developments for both the local Balinese and visiting international tourists alike. The abundance of fantastic restaurants that have sprung up has given guests so much to choose from. Basic hygiene and sanitation infrastructure has all but eliminated the old complaint of 'Bali belly'. The multitude of World-class hotels has lifted the island to the status of a World-class destination—in fact, in 2010, *Lonely Planet's Best of Travel* ranked Bali the second best place to visit among the World's top regions and in 2011 the prestigious *Travel and Leisure Magazine* chose Bali as the winner of their 'World's Best Island' category. Boutique shops, cafés, fine dining restaurants, discothèques and clubs are flourishing. Import companies now bring in almost anything you could desire and have made the island anything but the underdeveloped and backward place it was in the 1970's. Bali also abounds in just about every leisure and adventure activity you could expect to find in a tourist destination. All this has, of course, developed the local economy and given the Balinese people a wonderful chance to improve both their prospects and their standard of living. What is so extraordinary, however, is that the Balinese people, Balinese Hinduism and Balinese culture have actually been strengthened, not diminished, by tourism, as the island itself remains, at heart, what it was when I arrived 32 years ago.

Nigel Mason was born in Nottingham UK after his mother was evacuated out of London due to German bombing. After the War, he moved to Egypt with his father who was a British Army officer. Nigel attended boarding school in Surrey and grammar school in London. He left for Australia in 1959 with the Big Brother Movement to work on a farm in Victoria. After settling in Melbourne, Nigel moved on to the management of EMI Australia and later to a large musical industries store before arriving in Bali in 1980. Today, together with his Balinese wife Yanie, Nigel is the director of the world-renowned *Elephant Safari Park* in the mountains of north-central Bali and the owner of Bali's largest adventure company, Bali Adventure Tours. www.baliadventuretours.com.

Arjuna and Jakpacs

Dr. Pamela Noensie

Coming from my temporary home in The Hague, Holland in the 1970's, I remember my first lunch at *Murni's Warung*—a feast of rice surrounded by savouries called *nasi campur*, a salad with peanut sauce called *gado-gado* and black rice pudding. I was so engrossed with trying all the new tastes that I didn't notice my young son drifting away. When I discovered that he had gone, I quickly scanned the road wondering where a five-year old might go. Had he crossed the bridge to our small hotel?

Thankfully, before I panicked, someone told me my son was in Murni's boutique in the front of the restaurant. My question: how in the World did the Balinese lady get a scruffy young boy to try on a jacket?

I secretly watched as the lady pointed out secret pockets, and flipped the yellow jacket inside out to make a red backpack which she called a 'jakpac'. What a delightful, warm, attractive lady I thought.

The lady had a way of talking that 'blew my son's imagination'. She was explaining 'this would be a cool way to carry his arrows, bugs, and stones'. I listened as the lady told a story about the mythical hero Arjuna and his arrows. Still, I never imagined that the boy who disliked clothes might actually want to buy the jacket. However, to my surprise, he demanded enthusiastically: 'I want this jakpac!'

Who was this beautiful lady who could entice a five-year old boy to want to buy a jakpac? It was none other than the owner of the restaurant, Murni herself, and this was the beginning of a long, fun and surprising friendship.

Murni has guided me to not only some of my most memorable foods, but also on great walks like to the temple across the street and under the bridge from the restaurant where Murni, as a young girl, fetched water daily from the river and swept the temple clean.

Murni's impressive knowledge of Indonesian art and textiles has grown through the years. This often coincided with my own interests as I lectured on the Spice Island Cruise ships and studied art and textiles while living in Jakarta in the 1990's and, later, I taught in the same field in a university in the United States.

I now live in San Francisco and was delighted to see Murni and Jonathan in the Bay area a few years ago when Murni exhibited her museum-quality textiles and lectured at one of the Californian museums. In 2012, I enjoyed staying at *Murni's Houses* and visiting her impressive villa with four Californian friends. They loved Murni's traditional paintings, textiles and statuary, as well as her great new spa, *Tamarind Spa at Murni's Houses*.

In fact, this is a big reason I, like so many others, come back to Bali... to see Murni year after year. For me, and so many countless others from around the World, it is the lovely way she incorporates the new, while always honouring the fine arts and traditions of Bali.

Dr. Pamela Noensie is a scholar in the fields of psychology and communications. She lived in Indonesia for sixteen years, raising her family there (including operating an art gallery in Jakarta). She continues to spend half of her time in Asia. Pam has lectured extensively on the *Spice Island Explorer* cruise ships in the outer islands of Indonesia. She is the author of *Tari, the Little Dancer of Bali,* now in its second reprint. She currently lives in the San Francisco Bay Area.

You Must Order the Duck

Jonathan Copeland

Over a quarter of a century ago, in 1984 to be precise, I set foot in Bali. It took over twenty-four hours to arrive from London with scheduled and unscheduled stops in Paris, Geneva, Dubai and Jakarta and then a change of planes for Bali. Finally, exhausted and jet-lagged, I was in the busy, chaotic, smoke-filled terminal of Denpasar airport. I felt like Indiana Jones, an explorer, and in a way I was.

Old Balistas have been complaining since the 1930's that Bali has been spoiled by tourists, but to me nothing had been spoiled. I loved the ramshackled airport; I loved the people running round in circles like demented chickens; I loved the clouds of clove-scented *kretek* cigarette smoke. That's how airports should be. That's how they were.

The next morning I woke up in Kuta, a warm tropical paradise of multi-green vegetation, bright purple flowers, large orange butterflies and yellow birds, all a million miles from London and all waiting to be explored. Kuta 1984 is a far cry from Kuta 2014. In those days it was so laid-back it was horizontal. After five days it was time to get up. I got up to Ubud.

That was a journey and a half. Actually it was three journeys. I took the local *bemo* transport—rusty pick-ups full of women with vegetables, chickens and bright red lips and teeth or what was left of teeth chomping and chewing betel nut. They made me very welcome. After what seemed like a lifetime on the road I made my farewells and was dropped at *bemo* corner in Ubud.

I found my way to the *Tjampuhan Hotel* past farmers carrying huge bundles of grass for their cows and past the slippery waterfall that cascades down over the main road and still does. This was downtown Ubud. The *Tjampuhan Hotel* was THE place to stay. THE place to stay had no electricity except in the common parts and no hot water and no bath tubs, but it had charm and it had history and it had an abundance of insects and wildlife, most of which seemed to be occupying my room. The room was lit by a weak kerosene lamp, so they were out of sight, if not out of mind. Then, as now, the staff were as delightful as only the Balinese can be, despite an almost total lack of English. We got on fine.

It was not long before I had my torch in hand and was on my way out the Balinese double-door. Everyone carried a torch at night. By 6.30 pm it was pitch black. I crossed over the bridge and was soon delving into the menu at *Murni's Warung*, the only restaurant in town, an oasis of welcoming lights five minutes' walk away. Thatched roof, Dutch oil lamps, paintings on the walls, bamboo bar, bamboo bar stools, humorous *objets d'art*, bookcases, books for sale. This homely haven was the original *Murni's Warung*, which Murni started in 1974, and full of people, but they got me a table. Little did I know that that night would be a turning point in my life, not immediately, not for years, but a turning point nonetheless.

The menu featured Balinese Smoked Duck: order 24 hours in advance. Well, that sounded intriguing and order it I did. Next night, torch in hand, I was out the door, over the bridge, in the door, up at the bar, where a dark-eyed, dark-haired lady sat. 'I'm sorry, but there's a delay with the Smoked Duck. Would you like a glass of my mother's home-made Balinese wine on the house?' The way to a man's heart is through his stomach but his pocketbook is quicker. It wasn't long before the duck arrived and Murni and I had dinner together. For me, Bali is Murni and Murni is Bali. It was love at first bite.

Jonathan Copeland, Belfast boy, London lawyer, unrestrained in Ubud, bedazzled in Bangkok, is an audacious author and professional photographer, who authored *Secrets of Bali, Fresh Light on the Morning of the World* with Ni Wayan Murni, and was photographer for *Murni's Very Personal Guide to Ubud*, author and photographer of *Walking Tour of Rye, the most beautiful town in England*, author and photographer of *The Bangkok Story, an historical guide to the most exciting city in the World* and author and photographer with Ni Wayan Murni of *From Tattoos to Textiles, Murni's Guide to Asian Textiles, All You Need to Know... And More*. Jonathan's photography web site can be found at www.jonathaninbali.com. He also blogs with Murni at www.murnis.com.

Rose, Rose, I Love You

Rose Winkler

I first went to Indonesia in 1975 with Michael. I was his first girlfriend. I was seventeen years old. It was a seven-day Garuda package. Michael had fallen in love with me and I was soon to fall in love with Bali. We stayed at the newly opened *Grand Hyatt Hotel*, Nusa Dua and luxuriated on the beach. (It was long before the bypass and long sections of the road from Ngurah Rai Airport were unsealed.) We took a day trip to Kuta Beach and rode bicycles along the short section of single lane road—with deep open gutters—from *bemo* corner. My memory is that the 'road' ended just before *Mini-Seafood Restaurant*. Some 'Kuta Cowboys'— overly confident, handsome, buff young Balinese gigolos who spoke English with Australian accents, wolf whistled to me from the shade of a banyan tree at *bemo* corner—now long gone—and long forgotten. (Or perhaps they were trying to get Michael's attention because he was very good-looking and the boys were known not to have any particular preference.)

From where the asphalt abruptly ended, we followed a simple dirt track that meandered through the coconut groves across bridgeless streams to the whitewashed prison at Kerobokan—which at that time was in the middle of the *padi* fields. There were still bare-breasted young women bathing in the pristine rivers that flowed to the then deserted black sand beaches.

And like most visitors at that time, we took home bags of brightly coloured rayon *sarongs* and summer dresses, a carved wooden statue of an old fisherman casting a net, a painted *barong* mask, Indian-inspired silver jewelry and ... unfortunately, also 'Bali belly'.

Twenty years later my experience of Bali was very different. Together with my partner Alison and our husbands, we established *Alley-Rose Imports* and rode the crest of the Asian-style interior decorating wave—and then the Bali-inspired landscaping garden craze (it continues to be popular to this day).

I was the chief buyer for *Alley-Rose*. We were successful because I could read buyer trends—*Alley-Rose* had a knack of anticipating what people wanted to buy. And so we stayed ahead of the pack. (Many of our designs can still be seen in shops from Seminyak to Campuhan.) In those days, we worked closely with Agung Alit and his brother Degung Santikarma from Kesiman, who established *Yayasan Mitra Bali* to ensure that artisans in the rapidly expanding handicraft sector were receiving a fair price for their work and that they were using plantation products like *blalu* rather than old growth rainforest timber.

I remember one family in Tegalalang—a husband and wife. We were sourcing Balinese handicrafts at the time for

Oxfam stores and *Lifeline's Global Village* outlets. The young couple made these really gorgeous bamboo wind-chimes. We bought their entire year's inventory, thousands of them (people thought we were insane), and then placed another order for an equal number of units. Their offering price was, however, unacceptable and I told the young couple so. They looked so downcast—really crushed, until I explained that their price was unacceptably low. We sat with them for hours and taught them how to cost their labour and materials and determine a fair profit. We increased our offer to them by 50% (which made very little difference to our bottom line) but changed their lives. (And we sold every one of them.)

Because of the success of our handicraft and interior decorating lines we branched into garden furniture and landscaping features—and established *Heart of Stone Statuary*. (The name was inspired by my ex-husband.) We even shipped significant pieces to the United States where some still grace a private home that fronts one of the fairways at the *Rivera Country Club*, in Pacific Palisades, Los Angeles.

Most of our buying, however, was directly from producer families and communities in and around Ubud—and so the pattern of our lives was: early starts and breakfast at *Murni's Warung*, work and lunch at *Murni's Warung* and then a very long day and dinner at *Murni's Warung*—and it seemed like Murni was always there to welcome me—by name and song, *Rose, Rose, I Love You.*

Our business thrived through the tourism drought that accompanied the two Gulf Wars, the Asian economic collapse, the Bali bombings and the Chapelle Corby arrest and conviction. Often during those dark days for Bali we were literally the only ones in *Murni's Warung*—sometimes the only customers all day, yet it stayed open and the staff were all kept on. We created a jewelry line for *Alley-Rose* and many of the uniquely crafted items of gold and silver and ceramic were bought from *Murni's* shops, not just because the individual pieces were extraordinary and sold well but because we wanted to give something back by supporting Murni and her staff during some difficult times. And there was not a single day that Balinese Smoked Duck was not on the menu—regardless of how deserted Ubud was.

Rose Winkler is a high school teacher and now-retired businesswoman. She still travels to Bali for holidays. One of her favourite places to stay is *Murni's Villas* in the village of Samaon on the road from Ubud to Kintamani. ('Please make way for Rose', you can hear them say... from the famous song.)

Murni and Menschlichkeit

Dr. Rabbi Lennard Thal

It was 1994 and we were about to make our second trip to Asia, primarily to fulfill some rabbinic responsibilities in Singapore. The year before, one of our friends there showed us a clipping from the *New York Times* indicating that *Murni's Houses* should be included in a listing of 'the best small hotels in the World!' On this occasion, our two daughters (then nineteen and fourteen) were to be with us and we decided to include a side trip from Singapore to Bali and, recalling that piece from the *New York Times*, we made a reservation at *Murni's*. It wasn't—and isn't—a 'hotel'—it is both less and more! It is 'less' in that it is really a collection of small 'houses' and 'more' because it has the imprint of Murni on virtually every aspect of its premises and on the attention provided by the staff she has hired and supervised over the years.

Known to almost every longtime resident of Ubud—and deservedly so—we discovered then and on each of our many subsequent visits, that Ibu Murni (as many of the locals call her out of affection and respect) is a truly remarkable woman. It is not my tendency to use such descriptors loosely, so permit me to elaborate. Murni is intelligent, learned, loving, animated, inspiring, loyal to her Balinese roots and culture and deeply devoted to those of us lucky enough to become her friends. My wife and I are fortunate enough to be included in that circle and, indeed, we have spent time with her not only in Ubud but also in Bangkok and New York. Indeed, picture this—here is a woman with deep knowledge of textiles not only from Bali but elsewhere around Asia and we took her shopping for textiles in New York City just as she had accompanied us to Sideman (an hour or two from Ubud).

One way to gauge the quality of a person is to hear how those in that person's employ regard that person—and even the briefest of conversations with her staff—whether at *Murni's Houses* or at *Murni's Warung*—will reveal the almost reverential devotion they have for Ibu Murni. For example, both Tatik at the shop attached to the *Warung* and Kendri at the *Houses* have worked for Murni for something like twenty years (perhaps more) ... and they regard her as if she were their mother—or, at least, a loving auntie. After the unfortunate bombing on Bali some years ago, tourism fell off precipitously—yet Murni kept all of her employees since she was concerned about their livelihood, even if her own income stream was depleted at that time. I have come to see that that loyalty is more than reciprocated, especially in their concern about Murni's health in recent years when it has been necessary for her to spend significant periods of time getting treatment in Bangkok.

I would close with reference to two notions found embedded in Jewish tradition. One is that the quality we call

Menschlichkeit is to be prized—and as someone who cares so much for her dear friends and her own community, Murni embodies that quality without question. Secondly, in the Talmud we are taught that, at the time of the holy temple in Jerusalem 2,000 years ago, 'There are three crowns—the crown of Torah, the crown of the priesthood and the crown of kingship—but the crown of a good name is superior to them all.' No-one I know exemplifies the crown of a good name more than our dear friend Murni.

Dr. Rabbi Lennard Thal (A.B. Princeton; J.D. Stanford Law School, M.A.H.L., Rabbinic Ordination, D.D. Hebrew Union College-Jewish Institute of Religion) is the Senior Vice-President Emeritus of the (US) Union for the Reform of Judaism. He has served in a number of distinguished roles including Chief Development Officer and Director of Regions, Regional Director Pacific Southwest Council, Associate Dean of Hebrew Union College-Jewish Institute of Religion, Los Angeles Campus, as well as Visiting Rabbi (for the High Holy Days) at the United Hebrew Congregation of Singapore. After retirement he decided to take it easy and agreed to be Interim Director of the National Commission on Rabbinical-Congregational Relations.

Come back and have a Beer!

Wayne Lockwood

It was early January 1975. My girlfriend Karen and I had been to Bali the year before and had fallen in love with the island. We were studying filmmaking at college in Massachusetts and wanted to return to make a documentary. We prepared for a year—learning the language, studying the culture and readying ourselves for what ended up being two and a half years of adventure, fun, endearing friendships and hard work.

Armed with cameras, film, tons of equipment and the indefatigable optimism of youth, we set out. We knew about the history of Ubud and Campuhan as a major art and cultural center. This is where we wanted to be. For decades the Balinese had welcomed foreign visitors including artists, writers, actors, and celebrities with open arms. The welcome for us, the new *tamu*, proved to be just as gracious. (The Indonesian word for 'guest' is *tamu*.)

We had a letter of introduction to a German entrepreneur who lived in Penestanan with his Balinese wife and children. Penestanan is a village just past Ubud and Campuhan. (We weren't exactly sure how to get there.) Stowing our gear at the big hotel in Sanur Beach, we rented a motorbike and roared up the island, which, at that time, still had very little traffic and was mostly dirt roads and open rice fields. We were heading for we knew not what. It was getting late and the ride had been long. After passing through Ubud, and again heading down the hill, we came to a stop at a beautiful suspension bridge. It was single lane and painted a lovely silver color and it swayed ever so slightly. The Campuhan River flowed far below.

Wind-blown and weary from the ride, I looked to my left and there was a small, simple, charming, grass-covered pub with a few *tamu* sitting at the bar and a bevy of lovely young Balinese girls bustling about the place. I yelled out: 'Do any of you know where Walter (Foley) lives?' 'Yes' was the answer from an English gent. 'Just cross the bridge, go up the big flight of steps on the left and across the rice fields a couple hundred yards on you'll find him ... and after you do, make sure you come back and have a beer with us'.

Well, of course it turned out to be *Murni's Warung* and our home away from home for the next two or so years. Murni welcomed us so warmly and we all became good friends. Many a pleasant morning, afternoon and evening was spent there. Most days it was breakfast, lunch and dinner telling stories with friends. There was no electricity anywhere at that time. Beer and other drinks were in the cooler and ice was delivered by the ice man every morning. Food was cooked on a wood stove and light at night was provided by old kerosene-fueled Dutch lamps and handmade candles. Murni was the hostess with a half dozen village girls serving and cooking (with Murni keeping an eye on everything). The food was good and the beer cold (sometimes chilled with chunks of ice). Murni was so charming. She laughed and joked and told stories as good as any while making sure all was running smoothly and efficiently. She was such a great friend to us. I have so many memories of those wonderful times.

Bali has always attracted interesting characters—from all over the World. Many (or perhaps, most) stopping in at *Murni's* at some point in their visit—some staying. There were plenty of interesting Balinese too. One was Murni's father, who was a very funny man. He had a wry take on whatever happened to be going on that day. Many artists, photographers, writers, dancers and nomads came through; none missed the gaze of Murni's father.

So many evenings were spent at *Murni's Warung* drinking and swapping stories until late. When it was time to go we would stumble in the dark through the rice fields and moonlit paths to our homes and beds. We didn't need television or telephones (there were no cell phones in those days). It was Bali as it had always been. *Gamelan* music was to be heard everywhere and it would seem to drift far on the cool evening breeze. Balinese theater was also being performed—and it was just fine for a *tamu* to walk in, sit down and watch. We didn't have a care or a worry except for the long hike home on foot. 'Pick 'em up and put 'em down', I would repeat to myself like a mantra, quoting a favorite expression of a good friend.

I can't imagine our time in Bali without Murni and without *Murni's Warung*. Bali is magical—but having our special 'home away from home'—*Murni's*, made it all that more wonderful for us.

Wayne Lockwood has lived in Santa Cruz, California and Maui, Hawaii for the past thirty years where he has kept busy studying yoga, building homes and sailing. He produced *Light of Many Masks (1981)* with Karen Goodman. This documentary film looks at Balinese culture through the work of a master mask carver, and the *topeng* masked dance. He has one son—Westley and one daughter—Phoebe; they both speak words of Indonesian although neither has ever been there.

Terima Kasih, Murni

Sherry Davis

I was lucky enough to study dance in Bali in 1979. I first spent a week at a black sand beach in Java (took a *becak*, *bemo*, canoe and donkey cart to get there). While there, I picked up the rudiments of *Bahasa Indonesia* but, unbeknownst to me, also picked up malaria. Traveling in Java as a single woman at that time was rather challenging, so I soon took the wild night bus ride from Yogyakarta to Bali.

Ubud at that time was a true, small, artists' village—a dirt streets, no-running-water, no-telephones place. If you were walking down the road, someone across the street would ask where you were going and you would yell back—this was the village broadcast system. I was staying in a small thatched cottage above Campuhan and studying women's dance (the *Pendet*) with Ibu Sri and masked dance (*Topeng Keras*) with Pak Tutor.

I developed a fever and awoke one night with uncontrollable shaking. Everyone took such good care of me. They even offered me a natural remedy, which I think was pure quinine. All I know is that it had a nuclear green glow and one sip reduced me to tears. Luckily the medics were not far behind with pills, which were much easier to swallow.

During the week of my semi-delirium, I looked out my window to see the palm trees swaying in the wind with the same movement as a dancer's hands. Below me was a *sawah* and beyond that the river where the villagers came morning and night to bathe, filling the air with laughter and gossip. But the most magical event took place on the hill across the river. A temple was having its 100-year anniversary and that entire week I went to sleep and woke up to *gamelan* music. At last, I was on Bali time.

Bali time is such a relief from the hectic pace of the Western world. If I was late for a class, I would apologize profusely. The answer was always the same: *Tidak apa apa*— 'It's nothing.' One of the kindest expressions I know.

When I was able to move, I went to Ubud to a homestay with a mosquito net and where the Ibu would bring me hot water to mix with my *mandi* water to bathe. I was able to sit out at night with the women and children making offerings for the next day. I learned so much about Bali during these sessions. Once there was a praying mantis up by the light catching bugs and a woman said to me, *Lihat, Sherry, menari*. 'Look, Sherry, dancing.' Indeed, the mantis lifted his legs and turned his head with the exact movements of a *topeng* dancer. A little boy started humming a Balinese tune and we watching the dancing mantis.

I began my dance lessons again, but instead of *Topeng Keras* (which is the young warrior; *keras* meaning strong or hard) I had to switch to *Topeng Tua* (the more fragile old man)!

Bali was a very small community of villages then. No matter how far afield I traveled, when I told someone I had contracted malaria, invariably they would say, 'Ah, you should stay Ubud.' I traveled by *bemo* everywhere (there were no motorbikes and ubiquitous drivers offering their services). I met so many people and had such wonderful experiences. The Balinese, in addition to being very spiritual people, are also expert tricksters. You knew something was up when people around you got that 'cat that swallowed the canary' look on their face. Since Westerners were rare, they did not expect me to understand their language and often I was able to turn the trick back on them, to their delight.

It was when I moved to Ubud that I began frequenting *Murni's Warung*. It was one of only three restaurants in Ubud. The main selling point was that it was about the only place on the island where you could get fresh yoghurt. The other main selling point was Murni. She took me under her wing. She included me in visits to the fishing village to buy fish. She took me to the cookie 'factory', which consisted of old waffle irons on low wooden risers above wood fires. She was indeed my Ibu (Mother). Her kindness and generosity are well-known throughout the island. She is a shining example to women of how to be a Balinese businesswoman—always sharing beautiful Bali with her customers (which are really the wrong term because everyone ends up being her friend).

I hadn't seen Murni for a long, long time when I went to the *Arts of Pacific Asia Show* in San Francisco several years ago. The catalogue was very dense as it combined the *Tribal Arts* and *Textiles* Shows in one. I randomly opened the catalogue and it fell open to *Murni's of Bali*. It is such a large show that I might have gone through the whole exhibition and not seen her. I made a beeline to Murni's booth and had a tearful reunion. It had been almost thirty years since I had last seen her, but it felt like reconnecting with a long-lost family member. Indeed, I consider Murni family.

Seeing Murni again compelled me to return to Bali. Much has changed, although the beauty of the country and the sweetness (and mischievousness) of the people will never change. I was fortunate to stay at *Murni's Villas* for the first part of my trip and it was the perfect place to slow down again to Bali time and soak in the beauty of the island and the people. The minute you arrive, you feel part of the *Villas'* community. The staff are as nice as they can be. There are ancient stone carvings scattered across the property, lovely cloths and statues decorating the rooms, intricately carved doors, magnificent Balinese roofs, flowers and orchids everywhere, views of people working the rice fields—everything to delight the senses and calm the mind.

Terima Kasih, Murni. You and Bali are always in my heart.

Sherry Davis was born in the United States in Newport News, Virginia, and received her Bachelor's Degree in Theater from the College of Notre Dame of Maryland. She performed with repertory companies in Virginia (Norfolk Theatre Center and Chrysler Museum Actors' Theatre) before moving to West Coast of California. There, as a belated hippie, she lived in a tree house and pursued alternative acting experiences. This culminated in an improvisation/comedy troupe called *The Screaming Memes*. The troupe moved to San Francisco, California, and performed in the Bay Area for several years. In 1993, Sherry became the first woman Public Address Announcer for any major sport in the United States for the San Francisco Giants baseball team, for whom she announced for seven years (1993-1999) and is represented in The Baseball Hall of Fame in Cooperstown, New York. She now announces college women's basketball for St. Mary's College of California and does occasional theatre acting. Sherry makes her living as a legal secretary and longs to again return to Bali.

Ubud in a Rapidly Changing World

Dr. Rob Goodfellow

I honestly can't remember the first time I had a meal at *Murni's Warung*. The Ubud landmark seems as if it has always been part of my experience of Bali, a rich odyssey spanning over twenty-five years and some 200 visits.

And in the same way, I can't exactly recall my first introduction to Ibu Murni but place it somewhere in the slower, gentler, meandering world of the late 1970's.

My research on Ibu Murni, writing for the *Jakarta Post* in the 1990's, revealed that she was born just after World War II in the village of Penestanan-Ubud. Her life reflects the history of Ubud itself. Her family has always been closely involved with international travellers. Her mother cooked for Walter Spies, the German aristocrat painter, who lived during the 1930's in a thatched cottage overlooking rice terraces in the neighbouring village of Campuhan.

At this time (much like today), 'anyone who was anyone' visited Ubud and they all at some time ate Murni's mother's food: Charlie Chaplin, Noël Coward, Barbara Hutton, the Woolworths' heiress, Colin McPhee, the ethno-musicologist and his anthropologist wife Jane Belo, Vicki Baum, the novelist, as well as Margaret Mead and Gregory Bateson, the pioneering anthropologists.

Some of my colleagues have suggested that Miguel Covarrubias, the Mexican painter and ethnologist, was so inspired by the food in Ubud that he decided to write the still widely read and influential book *Island of Bali*, published in 1937, which in part inspired the must-read contemporary account of Balinese life and culture, *Secrets of Bali, Fresh Light on the Morning of the World* by Jonathan Copeland and Ibu Murni herself, published in 2010.

Colin McPhee likewise decided to stay and live in Ubud where he studied Balinese *gamelan* music. He wrote a marvellous book, *A House in Bali*, which has been reprinted in paperback. Murni's great aunt looked after him too.

In the 1950's it was in Murni's village of Penestanan that Arie Smit, a Dutch painter, founded a school of art called *The Young Artists of Penestanan* which has profoundly influenced the development of the *avant-garde* art for which the area is now known. Again Murni's family was involved.

During the 1960's, Ubud was not the bustling tourist centre it is today. I love to hear Murni's stories of how she would get up at 4 am every morning and cycle downhill to Sanur on the south coast of Bali and sell her textiles to visiting cruise ship passengers. If it was a bad day, she had to put her goods back on her head and cycle home up the hill to Ubud. However, before long, she had four shops in Sanur and counted the Rolling Stones' Mick Jagger as one of her regular clients. He is still a customer today.

By the mid-1970's Murni had returned to Ubud, where she created the first real restaurant in the area, *Murni's Warung*. Ever since, as far as I am concerned, it is one of THE places to go in Bali. Today *Murni's Warung* employs over sixty staff and continues to serve patrons from all over the World. It is the most romantic restaurant in Ubud. You can hear the sound of rushing water in the jungle gorge that has formed from the convergence of the River Wos and its tributary. Here locals and visitors, writers, artists and dancers all enjoy the atmosphere, the exotic cuisine and, most importantly—each other's company.

For the uninitiated, *Murni's Warung Shop* is actually located in the restaurant. It has been imitated but never surpassed for quality, authenticity and value. Her international clients, many of them being my friends too, think so highly of Murni that they call to check if she's in Bali before they book their flights. The *New York Times* has in fact named *Murni's Houses*, her travellers' accommodation in Ubud, as one of the best small hotels in the World and it now has a wonderful, healing spa, *Tamarind Spa at Murni's Houses*, in the grounds, which usually appears as the top spa, based on guests' experiences and reviews, in *Trip Advisor's Attractions in Ubud*.

It is however *Murni's Villas, Villa Kunang-Kunang*, that I call my favourite place in all of Bali (and probably the World). *Kunang-Kunang*, which means 'fireflies' in the Indonesian language, is about fifteen minutes' drive outside Ubud, on the road up to Mount Batur. The *Villas* look out over ancient rice fields and are set in three hectares of beautifully landscaped tropical gardens. Hidden away is a curved, infinity swimming pool, which merges into breath-taking views of the emerald-green rice terraces. There are fishponds, water-lily ponds, lotus ponds and the sounds of running water everywhere. The *Villas* are furnished with a mix of contemporary and antique Balinese and Indonesian furniture in Murni's inimitable style. There are walks along the rice terraces and, if Ibu Murni has time, she takes her friends and guests along trails where tourists never go, explaining the tropical trees, flowers and plants. Along the way she stops to introduce her guests to local people they would never otherwise get an opportunity to meet.

What continues to inspire Ibu Murni is her strong faith in the importance of maintaining Balinese culture as living and unique. This is combined with her genuine desire to extend friendship and hospitality to others and to show visitors a special piece of the real Bali. (Significantly, Murni's love of textiles has prompted her to initiate guided textile tours of the island.)

What continues to inspire me is that, in all the time since I have been visiting Ubud, I have found two constants in a rapidly changing, fast-moving and less personal world than those carefree days of late 1978: *Murni's Warung* and the gracious lady herself.

Dr. Rob Goodfellow is an author, writer, researcher and consultant. His specific expertise is in the field of identifying and managing risk associated with every level of international exchange—through briefings, advocacy, protocol training and the planning and the implementation of practical and appropriate strategies that minimise misunderstandings based on very different social and cultural perceptions. www.culturalconsulting.com.au.

My Favourite Mother

Janet de Neefe

"The story of my life is a long and complicated one," she said softly. And thus began my interview with the legendary Murni of *Murni's Warung* in Ubud.

Many of my fondest memories of Ubud in the Eighties are wrapped up in the walls of this multi-levelled eatery that is perched beside the Tjampuhan suspension bridge overlooking the Tjampuhan River. I remember spending oh-so-many lazy afternoons there when Ubud was a sleepy village, reclining in that tropical let-the-world-float-past way on creaky bamboo furniture. We'd sip on freshly squeezed lime drinks brimming with crushed ice while slowly eating *nasi campur* or *nasi goreng*. Lunchtimes drifted into dinner and it didn't matter. There was nothing urgent to be done except chat about life, love and cosmic heroes—there were no mobile phones, internet, emails, reality TV, not even Facebook! Life was suspended between our daily routine and the fairy-tale world of Indonesian mythology.

The ground floor pavilion of *Murni's Warung* was our preferred haven. Like the inner sanctum of a temple, this cosy space seemed magical and inspired discussions on all things sacred and profound. Ketut, my husband, any number of friends and I would gather at our favourite table and listen to never-ending tales of Ken Arok, one of the most powerful rulers of Indonesia in ancient times, the Mahabharata and the Ramayana. The tales would almost lull me to sleep as I listened to the ongoing treacheries, tragedies and majesty of Ken Arok, the extraordinary beauty of his wife Ken Dedes and Hindu epics recounting the sagas of family betrayal and bravery.

The seething jungle around us and the surging sound of the Tjampuhan River below enhanced the dramas. Nature seemed to grow before my eyes. I absorbed all that I could in what became a crash course in Indonesian history and Bali Hinduism.

Sitting with Murni in the downstairs Lounge Bar at *Murni's Warung* that has now replaced our favourite retreat, Murni chatted about her life, treading delicately through sad memories of her childhood that have laid deeply buried in her heart for so many years. But on this breezy day, they bobbed to the surface and floated around us as if we were in a time warp. In those days, life in Bali was often arduous, unforgiving and heartbreaking.

Murni touched on the violence that engulfed Indonesia in late 1965. She spoke of her own part in that story, of the nightmares that continued to haunt her for a long time afterwards and the wounds that have been patched superficially but never healed.

After three hours of emotional chatter, we dried our eyes together and steered the conversation back to the incarnation of *Murni's Warung*.

'I wanted my own business in Ubud so I rented this small *Warung* from Pak Munut. Victor Mason, who, believe it or not, is still alive and well in Ubud, gave it the name, *The Black Stump*. He said, just call it that and I did. But I had no idea what it meant!' she said.

'At first I had one bamboo table. I had started to sell *sarongs*, paintings and carvings. I didn't plan on having a *warung* and I am not at all a chef. My future husband Pat would sit in the shop with me. He wanted to drink beer and eat sandwiches so I made these for him. Guests who came into the shop would ask if they could buy some too.'

'I eventually opened a little kitchen and began to sell food and drink. Every morning I caught the *bemo* to Denpasar to buy tomatoes, cheese, ham and bread and would come straight back home to run the business. I borrowed beer from my mother who had a shop in the market. We made ice boxes from cement and filled them with ice.'

The following year in 1975, Murni bought the property and changed the name to *Murni's Warung*. Slowly the business expanded. Murni had clearly acquired the business acumen of her mother and the Cinderella-type childhood, living with her father's family in Denpasar, had prepared her for an around-the-clock hard-working shop-keeping routine.

'My guests taught me how to make everything. They taught me how to make guacamole because I had an avocado tree. But when they made it I couldn't eat it because it reminded me of a Balinese poultice they make here for pregnant women. We were the first in Ubud to make yoghurt. The culture was brought from Holland. I eventually bought a fridge and made jackfruit and white mango ice cream,' Murni reminisced.

But it's Murni's cakes that I loved the most and she was famous for them. In the Eighties you were lucky to find anything more than fried bananas on local menus.

Murni's Warung was one of the first to serve a selection of international sweet dishes to appease cake-eating, chocolate-craving gluttons like me. Her chocolate brownies and home-made sweet pies saved many a home-sick traveller.

Murni's Warung quickly became an institution and remains so to this day. It is an Ubud icon. Back then, I remember that one of the greatest joys about visiting *Murni's Warung* was simply Murni. She used to sit at the front desk and invariably wander up to your table and have a chat. When Murni wasn't there holding the fort, Nyoman, the head cashier and part of the family, took her place. Nyoman was a girl with her own brand of dry humour but that's another story. But it was Murni we all wanted to see.

There is so much to love about Murni. Whether it be her heart that's as big as the moon, her gentle nature, grace or soft humour ... or the combination of these matched by her lovely soft round face ... whatever it is, it's infectious.

Murni's moving tale of longing, separation and hardship stays with me. Her struggles and subsequent battles laid the foundations of her success. She has learned to straddle two cultures, for better or for worse, and created an iconic business, single-handedly, that helped put Ubud on the map. And for all these reasons, and for many more, she is and will always be one of my favourite mothers in town.

Janet de Neefe was born in Melbourne but has lived in the 'magical mountain kingdom of Ubud' for nearly three decades. She fell in love with Bali on her first visit in 1974 and then she fell in love with her husband, Ketut, and moved to Ubud in 1984. She is the founder of the Ubud Writers and Readers Festival and author of *Fragrant Rice and Bali: The Food of My Island Home*. She is the owner of two restaurants—*Casa Luna* and *Indus*, a bar, a homewares shop, a cooking school and a guest house. www.ubudwritersfestival.com and www.casalunabali.com.

The Pioneer Interviews the Pioneer

Bill Dalton

In the 1609 version of Shakespeare's *Sonnet 54* the Bard writes: *If their bee nothing new, but that which is, Hath beene before, how are our braines beguiled.*

William Shakespeare here may well have been a travel writer. I say this because specialising in the largest archipelago state in the World, in an accurate, complete and fair manner, has certainly kept my *'braines beguild'* for coming up to forty years.

The story of how I founded Moon Publications in a youth hostel in Queensland in 1973, with the publication of the often called 'ground-breaking' *Indonesia Handbook*, is well known. I have always had a special interest in Southeast Asia. During the past twenty-six years, for example, I have explored over 100 of Indonesia's 17,000 islands. What is less appreciated is that, at last count, my travel writing has taken me to some eighty-one countries around the World, now mostly working as a so-called 'anonymous free agent'.

I like being a well-informed and experienced observer and evaluator of travel destinations and services without anyone being aware of what I'm doing. Several times I've taken extensive notes while eavesdropping on travelers who are exchanging travel impressions and information as they sit around an adjacent table in a restaurant. I also love learning about weird subjects that I would not ordinarily ever care about or pursue. When you write travel, you write about every topic under the sun—history, religion, ethnography, music, the arts, biology, economics—you name it. It's a profession the pursuit of which makes for a well-rounded education.

And so it is with Murni. As an 'anonymous free agent' writing for the Bali Advertiser, I interviewed the woman I consider to be one of the pioneers of tourism in Bali—and who, like the example of *Indonesia Handbook*, created something which, to misquote the Bard, *Hath [not] beene before*.

Bill Dalton: Tell me about your background?

Murni: I come from a long line of hard-working Balinese ladies. I think I must be a reincarnation of one of them. I was born in the small village of Penestanan, just after the war. My mother was from Penestanan and my father was from Campuhan, the neighbouring village. I lived in Penestanan until I was five years old and then we moved to Campuhan. My restaurant and shops are in Campuhan, so I haven't really come very far!

Bill Dalton: What was your early childhood like?

Murni: Very hard, like it was for all Balinese in the Fifties and Sixties. Until I was four years old, my mother used to carry me on her hip as she went from house to house offering salt, dried fish and things like that. She wasn't selling; she was bartering. In those days she used to offer her goods in return for rice. I think I learnt to bargain watching her at that young age. My parents split up when I was seven and I went to live with my aunt in Denpasar. When I was twelve, I returned to my mother in Ubud.

Bill Dalton: What was the first enterprise you started?

Murni: I made my first money when I was living with my auntie. I had to get up at 2 am to make cakes for morning coffee. Then I had to go to the houses of the Balinese and Chinese families in Denpasar and sell the cakes. The money went to my aunt, but, if I sold all the cakes, she gave me five rupiah. I had to save two rupiah for my school books, which left me three rupiah for lollipops. As I said, when I was twelve, I went back to Ubud and lived with my mother. She was then a very successful business woman. I worked with her in the market for two or three years and started my first business in 1961, cycling down to Sanur to sell batik to the tourists. That started my love of textiles and beautiful things.

Bill Dalton: How did you discover which products or services appealed specifically to the tourist market?

Murni: I watched their eyes. If they opened their eyes wide, they liked the goods and I had a buyer. It was then just a matter of price. I always give very fair prices, so my customers come back. I still have customers from those days. I also discovered that quality is more important than anything. People remember quality. As regards the restaurant, I think I just knew instinctively that cleanliness, friendly service and good lavatories are really important.

Bill Dalton: How many businesses do you own right now?

Murni: Far too many. I should be retired by now. Apart from the restaurant and shops, there's *Murni's Villas* and *Murni's Houses*. We've also got into the wedding business. Weddings and honeymoons in *Murni's Villas* are very popular. I really enjoy those. My web site, www.murnis.com, is also thriving. It's probably the largest Bali web site and growing all the time. [Since this interview, she's now created the leading Spa in Ubud: *Tamarind Spa at Murni's Houses*!].

Bill Dalton: Of all your different enterprises, which gives you the most satisfaction?

Murni: Hard to say. I like different aspects of all of them. I love meeting old and new friends in the restaurant. I enjoy the shops, showing people my collections and exchanging ideas about textiles and antiques. I also get a lot of pleasure travelling, not just abroad, but also in this country.

Bill Dalton: Which business is the most difficult to run?

Murni: Easy! The restaurant, but it's a lot of fun.

Bill Dalton: What difficulties (or strokes of good luck) did you encounter in the early days starting *Murni's Warung*?

Murni: It's pretty difficult running a restaurant with no electricity or refrigeration. I did that for six years. It's also difficult getting up at four in the morning to go down to Denpasar to get supplies and back in time to serve breakfast. Thank God those days are over.

I had many strokes of luck. I met really nice people in the restaurant who taught me fabulous recipes and we had great laughs trying them out. Many are still on the menu. Every day I meet interesting people from all over the World who teach me a lot about antiques and handicrafts.

Bill Dalton: What makes *Murni's Warung* different from other similar restaurants in Ubud?

Murni: I built the first restaurant in Ubud, so I was able to choose the best spot. The location and atmosphere are very special. It sits on a gorge overlooking the Campuhan river, which you can hear rushing below. It's a sacred river. I don't think any restaurant is quite so romantic. I also keep everything traditionally Balinese—from the food and décor to the costumes of the waiters and waitresses.

Bill Dalton: How do you relieve stress?

Murni: I play the *gamelan* really hard!

Bill Dalton: What is the most valuable antique object you own?

Murni: Myself!

Bill Dalton: What would you like to be doing now?

Murni: Having dinner with Walter Spies in *Mrs. Balbir's Indian restaurant* in Bangkok.

Bill Dalton is a travel writer, adventurer and founder of *Moon Publications*—a collective of world travelers and writers. The company started with travel guides to Asia and later became the top publisher of guides to the Americas. Moon was an early advocate of independent travel, and their authors often live in the areas they write about. The Moon Handbooks series has since become known for its award-winning, well-written and exceptionally informative travel guides. www.moon.com.

Food of the Gods on the Island of the Gods

Janice Carson

In the 1970's, my husband Larry and I bought an around-the-World airline ticket and travelled for five wonderful months. Before the era of globalization, the World was a very different place. We experienced so many cultures that were yet to be changed by mass tourism. When we arrived in Bali, we simply fell in love. In those days, Kuta was a quiet fishing village with an outdoor market right on the beach. We stayed in a bungalow by the ocean for a few dollars a night. We both felt that we had died and gone to heaven. There was so much magic all around us.

We would hear the sound of a *gamelan* playing and follow it back to a village. We would witness *kris* dancers in trance, seemingly turning their swords in on themselves. We would be the only outsiders there and we could hardly believe what we were seeing. There were no paved roads at that time, so a trip by open truck or *bemo* to Ubud was a long, bumpy ride. We were packed in with chickens, piglets and betel nut chewing ladies with blood red grins. It was wonderful.

When we arrived in Ubud, we were enthralled by the natural beauty of the landscape and the greenery of the terraced rice fields. The people were so elegant and dignified. There were only a few small places to stay on Monkey Forest Road and fewer places to eat. We walked everywhere and discovered a beautiful *warung* overlooking a river. It was called *Murni's Warung*. We were introduced to real Balinese dishes like *Bebek Tutu* and *Babi Guling*. We were treated to black rice pudding with grated coconut. To eat the 'food of the gods' on 'the island of the gods' was almost a sensory overload!

Almost thirty years after our first visit, while again enjoying a wonderful *Bebek Tutu* at *Murni's Warung*, we were approached by Murni herself. She asked if we had met. We had indeed, only it was twenty-five years earlier—when we had stayed at *Murni's Houses*. We were surprised she remembered us and we asked her to join us for dinner. When Murni discovered that I had been a buyer of tribal art and textiles for the past quarter of a century, she offered to show us her private collection. I was very impressed with the rarity and quality. Many of her pieces were museum standard.

I told her about the San Francisco *Arts of Pacific Asia* and *Tribal Art and Textiles Shows* that take place once a year. These are highly vetted showcases of some of the World's best art and textile dealers' private collections. Murni was very excited about the prospect of visiting the United States. I told her she would be welcome to stay with us and I would be happy to help her. The problem Murni had was with current values of her rarest artefacts. By the time she arrived, I had assembled several experts to give a consensus on each item. It was a wonderful day. We listened while the merits of each piece were debated. We then celebrated with a glass of champagne and a wonderful lunch. Murni was glowing.

Needless to say, the shows were a great success. It turned out that Murni knew hundreds of people and so it really was more like a reunion. Everyone had a story about meeting Murni or staying at her *Villas*. It was then that I understood how she could remember us after all those years. Murni remembers every moment of her remarkable life. She just loves people and is in fact the most social person I have ever met.

We have been back to Bali every year since those gentle times. We have seen so much change, but the one constant remains—it is *Murni's Warung*. It is still the place where travellers meet over fabulous traditional dishes in a beautiful setting.

Janice Carson graduated from the San Francisco Art Institute in 1974 with a degree in sculpture. She then began travelling the World collecting art, artefacts and textiles from throughout Indonesia, Africa and New Guinea. After twenty-two years as buyer and manager, she retired and immediately started her own business designing and producing jewelry in Bali. In 2006, Janice and her husband Larry established the *Ganesha Foundation* for the education of some of Bali's neediest children. www.ganeshafoundation.org. Photograph by Jonathan Copeland.

Dark Memories of Indonesia

Jason Schoonover

My first trip to Indonesia was in 1979. It was so disappointing that I swore I would never return— and I didn't for a third of a century. I had my pocket picked while getting off a mini-van on my way up to Mount Tangkuban, West Java, and I was surreptitiously targeted by a gang of young thieves on the train.

One of the gang struck up a 'friendship', wanting me to help him practise English. Out of 'gratitude' he bought me a 'chocolate' from one of the vendors working the aisle. The train ride was interminable. It was hot and humid and airless. John Fowles' *Magus* was fascinating, but dense. Growing sleepy, I leaned into the window for a nap. I remember my new friend waking me, supposedly to 'see something interesting' outside. Through what appeared to be a thick fog I could make out two tense young men sitting opposite. It didn't seem right. Then I was out again. When I was shaken awake at the terminal I was lying prone on the seat. My fellow passengers were gone. In a muddle I realized something was seriously wrong; I did a clumsy inventory. My camera and cash were stolen but fortunately I still had my traveler's cheques and passport.

My next memory was of somehow managing the steep steps from the train and somehow getting onto the ferry and somehow arriving in Kuta from the port terminus. My last memory was a crowd of backpackers rushing towards a guesthouse check-in seeking rooms—and me raising my voice that I desperately needed to lie down. Seeing my distress some fellow passengers and the proprietor quickly led me to a bed, into which I plunged. I arose from my stupor twelve hours later.

Welcome to Bali.

I was not a freshman traveler. The year before I had soloed around the World, including traversing the fabulous Asia Overland Trail from Istanbul, through Iran, Afghanistan, the Khyber Pass and down into Sri Lanka, where I pieced together a major *Devil Dance* collection which was acquired by Vancouver's *Museum of Anthropology*. (I had more than paid for my trip by stringing travel stories to sixteen Canadian newspapers and several American publications, including the *LA Times*, *SF Chronicle* and *Boston Globe*.)

Since I was in Bali, I tried to make the best of a lousy start and, after linking up with a couple of Australian girls from Melbourne (whom I had kicked around with in Singapore), we rented motorbikes and headed up inland. Our first stop was Ubud, then a small quiet village. We stayed at a simple place down by the old Dutch Bridge. I remember being much impressed with the gorge and registering the serenity, the quiet drip of rainwater from the elegant areca palms, the lazy hum of insects, and the artistic atmosphere. But I was still bummed out by my experience in Java and not much else filtered through. I didn't trust anyone, and being cautioned that thieves worked the *losmen* every night didn't help my earned paranoia. We continued on to Lovina—where I was impressed with the beach—but by then I'd had enough. I headed back to Kuta, changed my ticket and flew on to Sydney swearing I'd never return or, for that matter, ever write a single travel article about Indonesia.

And I didn't return, rather establishing myself in Bangkok. After my second ethnological collection was sold to the *Smithsonian*, I was launched on a fascinating career that ranged all over Southeast Asia (minus Indonesia) including the Himalayas and Sri Lanka where I collected significant anthropological collections for museums around the World. I developed a reputation as an adventurer and was elected as a Fellow of *The Explorers Club*—all of which I fed into my adventure-thrillers.

In 1987, Bantam Book's President flew me to New York for consultation on *The Bangkok Collection*, which they published internationally as *Thai Gold*. While high in her office overlooking Fifth Avenue, my publisher gave me a copy of a book that they were also publishing that she thought I might be interested in. It was *Ring of Fire* by the Blair brothers. I was impressed and I still have that book today.

The sour taste I had for Indonesia would have remained except for Su Hattori. The Imperial Dragon Lady and I have been happily unmarried since 1988 and she always wanted to see Bali. I resisted until several of our Bangkok friends visited and returned with stars in their eyes and awe in their voices. I had run out of places to explore in fascinating, exotic Southeast Asia; and, by this time, ethnology was becoming a little thin on the ground—so I took a deep breath and nodded. We booked tickets from Bangkok in January 2012.

A third of a century has changed me—and it certainly has changed Ubud. The quiet hamlet that tweaked my interest was gone and had splurged into an international tourist destination. Just the same, denizens hadn't become jaded like in so many other places, and I quickly appreciated the soft, gracious, positive manner of the Balinese. The artistic sense and lifestyle that is so refined and unique to Bali that had captivated so many of our Bangkok friends now belatedly began to enchant me too. It enveloped Madame Su from the moment we arrived.

One of my first stops was back to the river gorge near the bridge. I was intrigued to see *Murni's Warung* near the same spot I had stayed at so many years ago. Being from Bangkok, I would be lying if I said I didn't know something about bars and *Murni's Lounge Bar* is one of the finest watering holes anywhere—a gem.

Su and I heard about *Murni's Warung* through friends of friends and were surprised to find the complex tumbling elegantly into the gorge with the bar and restaurant nearest the water. To our surprise, we were greeted warmly by the hostess herself—Ni Wayan Murni—and, at her invitation, we joined her and Jonathan Copeland, her co-author on *Secrets of Bali*, for a tall, cool drink. We quickly learned that we shared a great deal in common—from collecting textiles and ethnology to living in Bangkok.

For Su and I, Ni Wayan Murni epitomizes everything we have experienced about Balinese people: a warm, gracious, relaxed, sensitive and polite culture. I realized I had been unlucky thirty-three years previous. (Today, it is well-known that con men and tricksters work the night buses and trains with rohypnol treats all over East Asia.) The trip has rather opened a vast new area of Southeast Asia for me to explore. There might even be some ethnology on remote islands left to collect and store in museums where it will be safe and saved for posterity.

And I'll be back to Bali. Java, however, may still take some time....

Jason Schoonover, Fellow Emeritus of *The Explorers Club*, was educated at Vancouver's Simon Fraser University (English, History) and has been a writer and an ethnologist since the 1970's. As a field collector, his anthropological collections are found in museums around the World, as well as private collections. South and Southeast Asia, including the Himalayas, are his main areas of interest. A one-time columnist, he is widely published in newspapers and magazines and has a further background as an announcer and writer/director/producer in Canadian radio, television and stage. He founded Schoonover Properties in 1975. He was profiled in Jerry Hopkins' *Bangkok Babylon: The Real-life Exploits of Bangkok's Legendary Expatriates are often Stranger than Words* and featured in Maryann Karinch's *Business Lessons from the Edge: Learn How Extreme Athletes use Intelligent Risk Taking to Succeed in Business*. His books, both fiction and non-fiction, are in the adventure field. He and 'The Imperial Dragon Lady', Su Hattori, divide their time between Bangkok, Saskatoon, Canada, and the rest of the World. Exploring old Canadian fur trade and exploration routes by canoe is one of their passions. www.jasonschoonover.com and www.jasonschoonover.com/blah.html.

How We Met Murni

Meitie (Cornelia) Bock

It must have been around the late 1970's. My husband Herbert, who was a student at that time, and I had not long been married in Vienna and it was our second trip to my home country, Indonesia. On our first visit we didn't manage to visit *The Island of the Gods*, but on our second we had saved enough money to make the trip from Jakarta, where my parents lived.

It was an adventurous bus journey from Surabaya to Ketapang—to say the least. The bus broke down twice; then we had to wait, all fifty or so passengers, in the middle of the road and in the middle of the night, for another vehicle. We were then crammed into an already full relief bus. (I ended up with a very tall Frenchman and his surfboard on my lap.) From there a ferry took us over to Gilimanuk, Bali. It was a rough crossing too.

We were then carted off to Denpasar, which in those days had almost no hotels. We had not made any reservations, anywhere, so we were dumped, at 1 AM, into what later on turned out to be a so-called 'hour hotel'. I'll leave the rest up to your imagination.

The next morning we fled, truly, we ran way. Fortunately, we managed to find a cute little inn in what is now Seminyak. The people were lovely but breakfast was non-existent so we had some *kue basah* and *pisang goreng* at the local market, served and eaten with a huge glass of Bali coffee under a banyan tree. Soon all the local *bemo* drivers knew Herbert— the foreigner who liked his coffee black and sweet! (At night there were *legong* dances, right in front of our hotel room, that lasted till around 2 AM.)

There were no more than three big hotels anywhere in Bali at the time. There was not yet a highway and roads were really just paved tracks. When we asked for directions, the answer was usually a friendly but vague... 'after the third coconut tree go north, and then go east after you see the temple....' Maps were almost non-existent and most Balinese spoke only Balinese, so, at that time even for me, an Indonesian, it was very hard to understand and be understood.

We rented a motorbike and one of our first trips was to discover Bali inland. We had been driving around in the area of Tampaksiring for what seemed to us a very long time with no *warung* anywhere where we could buy ourselves something to eat. We were hot and thirsty and becoming desperate.

We took the road from Payangan (passing by what is now *Murni's Villas*) and soon enough we saw the first signs that we were nearing a village. Ubud at that time consisted of more or less one road—*Jalan Raya*. Campuhan Road, now full of hotels and restaurants, was a small dirt thoroughfare flanked only by *padi* fields and bamboo woods.

On the lookout for a *warung*, we drove around a sharp curve (where the Neka Museum now stands), passing by what is now the Tjampuhan Hotel, and that is when we saw in front of us the beautiful old wood and steel suspension bridge over the river. Herbert had to slow down so as not to slip and, right after that, was a sight for tired eyes (and hungry stomachs). It was *Murni's Warung*—a small wooden building with smoke coming out from what must have been the kitchen, wooden planks, stools and tables in front and a few racks with the most beautiful coloured batik clothes (Murni always had taste); and there was the smell of food and coffee. To our surprise, there in the middle of the street, too lazy to stand up even when we approached on our motorbike, were some all-white Bali dogs stretched out in the sun.

We stopped and, when we sat down, out came a smiling Murni. She then offered us the best *nasi campur* we had ever eaten, followed by a plate of hot and crispy *pisang goreng* and huge cups of steaming black Bali coffee.

Murni, you saved our lives. This was the start of our lifelong friendship.

Meitie (Cornelia) Bock was born in Bandung, Indonesia. At the age of four she moved with her family to Jakarta where she eventually studied Psychology at the University of Indonesia. In 1970, she moved to Vienna, Austria, where she worked for The United Nations Industrial Development Organization (UNIDO) for over thirty years. Since retirement, she and Hebert are hardly in Vienna, enjoying their mutual passion for travelling. Their apartment is covered with textiles from all over the World, including some special pieces from Murni's collection.

Reflections of a Mountain Man

Rupert Pullee

I hail from the opposite side of the globe to Bali. *The Pen-Y-Gwryd Hotel*, of which I am co-proprietor, is located in the pass at the head of the rugged Nantygwryd and Nant Cynnyd rivers in Gwynedd, North Wales. It is flanked by the majestic Glyder range and is close to the foot of Mount Snowdon—the highest peak in England and Wales. Few places—anywhere in the World—could claim a more breathtaking location; or so I thought. That was until I stayed at *Murni's Villas*, situated in the cool, central highlands of the island of Bali and had the extraordinary opportunity of having lunch with Murni herself.

As a 'mountain man' myself, I am attracted to high places, so perhaps it is not really a coincidence that I made my way to Ubud. And as a hotelier, I am in a good position to describe food. Let me tell you that the aroma of coffee was the first sign of the good things to come. Grown by local villagers—I could actually smell the beans as I drove up the road to the Villa—the local product tastes different from other varieties of Balinese or Javanese coffee.

The appetiser of fresh yoghurt and honey was a taste sensation. I understand that a friend of Murni's created the 40-year-old culture and passed the secret on to her. The honey is dark in colour and piquant in taste. It is collected by hand from wild hives that thrive on the myriad of fragrant flowers that bloom almost all year round—frangipani, hibiscus and honeysuckle.

The Ubud region is famous for some of the most exotic fruits on earth—a veritable Garden of Eden of mangoes, rambutans, papaya, mangosteens and lychees, which were planted in the Payangan area in the early 19th century. Murni actually asked me to describe the gorgeous taste of the mangosteen—a deep purple, soft-shelled fruit that can be opened by hand to reveal pure white, individual fleshy segments. Guests have variously described the fruit, which overflows an antique bowl in the middle of the breakfast table, as a blend of pear, banana, strawberry, apple, passionfruit, and honeydew melon.

Murni's breakfast specialty, however, is *bubur mebasa*. *Bubur* means 'porridge' in Indonesian; *basa* means 'spice' in Balinese. This is considered an everyday Balinese breakfast for locals but was an amazing delicacy for me. The dish is both nutritious and sustaining. It was impossible to refuse a second (and even a third) helping.

My palate was then refreshed with a selection of fresh juices—avocado, tomato, orange, mandarin or tropical lime with crushed ice. *Salak*, an indigenous fruit with an exterior resembling snakeskin—easily peeled by hand—exposes a firm, crisp flesh that defied further description but seemed to encourage conversation as the bowl of fruit emptied and the bowl of discarded skins overflowed. Fresh jackfruit coated with a thick ginger sauce is a fitting final temptation.

And then it was off to *Murni's Warung* for dinner. Should I describe that too? No, I think you are going to have to experience it for yourself.

Rupert Pullee is the co-proprietor of the *Pen-y-Gwryd Hotel*—one of the most famous hotels in the World and the 'home' of British Mountaineering. Before going into 'the family businesses' (whose international reputation was established by his grandfather Chris Briggs OBE) Rupert studied hotel management in Manchester and worked and travelled in the United States and Australia. www.pyg.co.uk.

Om Shanti Shanti Shanti Om

Forsheeza Jolly

It was 2002 and I was thirteen years old. I was pulled from school in Australia to be a volunteer for an exhibition of textile and fibre art called *Tracking Cloth*. I actually helped set it up in Denpasar before it went on to Yogyakarta and Jakarta the same year when it was my brother's turn to volunteer. (I had already spent a lot of time in Yogyakarta where I went to a local school with Simon while my Dad was teaching.)

My job was to wear white gloves and take directions. It was an amazing time. Lots of adventure and even high drama as the exhibition organisers, politicians and diplomats struggled to convince Customs to release the exhibition from the bonded store at Ngurah Rai International

Airport. The 'special fee' they were demanding was many times more than the actual budget of the project. A signed letter from the Governor of Bali was even ignored. They were untouchable. There was a lot of sitting around in the heat while we waited for something, anything, to happen. I think Yanie Mason felt sorry for me and invited me to stay with her and Nigel for a week.

But ... at five minutes to 5 pm on the last possible day before the exhibition could be mounted, a minor miracle happened: Indonesian Customs completely lost interest and said, 'Do whatever you want, we don't care anymore'— so, the exhibition director commanded, 'Break the seals and open the boxes.' *Tracking Cloth* was amazing. Even the Indonesian President saw the exhibition and said in the press that, 'It has created a symbol of goodwill between our two neighbouring nations.'

It was also good luck that my *Tracking Cloth* time coincided with *Nyepi*—the Balinese day of silence, sort of Balinese New Year. My Dad and I were staying at *Murni's Villas* in Samaon near Kintamani at the time; and because we were with Ibu Murni, we were involved in everything— especially our own private *Ogoh-Ogoh*. Ibu Murni explained that it was important that I help her frighten the demons away from the *Villas*; why not? Of course I'm going to do that. So, Ibu Murni, her two dogs, Toby and Buwung, and my Dad and Nyoman and Kadek had this incredible time, making noise, firing off skyrockets, yelling and whooping and shouting and marching along paths with flaming torches. We even banged some old dustbin lids together. In the village we could see the flash of explosions made by kids who were lighting acetylene gas in big bamboo tubes. It was anarchy. I loved it.

Ibu Murni said that because the next day was *Nyepi* we all had to follow these instructions: *Amati Geni*—No fires or lights; *Amati Karya*—No physical work; *Amati Lelungan*—We were not to go out on to the road; and *Amati Lelangguan*—

there was to be no TV or telephone or DVDs or internet or gameboys.

On *Nyepi*, everything was closed. There was not a single car or motorbike on the roads. All the shops and stalls and markets were deserted. Nobody cooked or went outside. We just lay around all day and all night and read and talked and had some really great snacks—just Ibu Murni and my Dad and I. It was like the clock had been turned back thousands of years. The birds went crazy like they had been waiting all year for a bit of peace and quiet. At night the sky was full of stars and fireflies and the sounds of frogs. I could hardly believe it and neither could Toby and Buwung, who got about a whole year's patting in one day.

Ibu Murni said, 'Kate, *Om Shanti Shanti Shanti Om*,' and I replied, 'Happy Balinese New Year, Ibu.'

The next day everything was back to normal, although, after I had experienced the day of silence, I couldn't help thinking how awesome it would be if we could have *Nyepi* more than once a year—say once a week or at least every few months, and not just in Bali.

I nearly forgot. I lost a tooth on *Nyepi*. It just fell out. Ibu Murni wrapped it up in a small piece of white cloth and put it into a handmade jewelry basket and said to treasure it and that it would always remind me of Bali.

Forsheeza Jolly is the stage name of Kate Goodfellow. Kate studied acting at the Australian Theatre for Young People and at the National Institute for the Dramatic Arts. She is a graduate of Actors Centre Australia. She currently lives in a share house in London. Photograph by Walter Maurice.

My Home in Bali

Jim Omi Cramer

We first arrived in Bali in 1974, the very first year that *Murni's Warung* opened. We were living in a grass hut or *pondok* on a local Balinese farm, on the ridge across from the old Dutch bridge and up past the *Tjampuhan Hotel*.

We mostly ate at local food stalls or *warungs* to save money but our big treat was to wander down the hill to *Murni's* for the famous chocolate cookies or Pat's equally famous 'Upper Elk Valley Burgers'.

In those days, kerosene lamps lit the houses and the restaurant. We would meander to *Murni's Warung* and arrive just before dark when our Balinese neighbours were batheing in the river. You could hear the laughter and joking as we crossed over the bridge. After dinner and in the dark, we would follow our flashlights back to our shack (which eventually became a house).

We hosted Murni and Pat at our house, with, as Murni would say, 'The best view in Bali'—*Gunung Agung*, the Mother Volcano in the distance, the long grass or *alang-alang* covering the hillside with the river quietly flowing below.

After lunch we would go for a swim. Only Murni would join us. Pat wasn't the swimming in the river type. In fact, he was very reclusive but Murni did get him up to our house at least once.

As the years went by, we often met Murni and went in search of the perfect *durian* or would take hikes to the Monkey Forest at Sangeh. Murni was always such a wonderful, kind, generous hostess—and she still is today.

Our daughter was born in 1977 and Morny, Murni's daughter, a year later. This bonded together our two families. We would often walk to *Murni's* to have lunch or dinner and let our daughter visit and play with Morny. I remember fondly that we all had to walk over the dog, Dausa (I think that was his name) who sat at the front door to welcome us all. And of course, Murni's dad was always a part of the scene.

Before 1980 there were only a handful of 'tourists' living in Ubud, or even visiting, as it was very difficult to get to in those days, having to cross all the one-way suspension bridges. I long for those simple days, with fireflies hovering over the dark road, the ducks following the 'magic wand' held by the Balinese farmer, the distant, hypnotic sounds of the *gamelan* drifting through the warm still night, the sound of the *kulkul* calling everyone to the *pura* and the graceful presence and beautiful welcoming smile of Murni. We were all so lucky to share that magic time together. Recalling those happy days of long ago has given me the opportunity to revisit some truly wonderful times in Bali.

Jim Omi Cramer is an author, traveller and owner of the *Bali Advisor*, a web site offering free advice for travellers to Bali.

He produced the travel video *Impressions of Paradise* narrated by Herbie Hancock and wrote the guide book *Impressions of Paradise: Suggested Itineraries around the Island of Bali*. Currently living in Santa Rosa, California, Jim also heads the office for *Spirit Tours*, leading spirit based tours from Bali to Bhutan and beyond. www.baliadvisor.com and www.spirit-tour.com.

Rest, Recuperate and Recharge

Jayne Ward

In January 1975, just after celebrating my 18th birthday, I flew to Denpasar, Bali—alone, since none of my friends had the money to join me. I felt both liberated and excited at the opportunity of travelling, especially to a country with so many things to see and do and learn and experience; and one so culturally different from and yet so geographically close to Australia.

It was a time when much was believed about Australia's neighbour Indonesia—but little was known.

(As luck would have it, at the time, our exchange rate was very favourable and so my savings lasted marvellously.)

I actually sat on the plane with a lady who was a university lecturer from Hawaii and she invited me to stay in her suite at the *Bali Beach Hotel*. So I had fallen on my feet as they say. This was the only international standard hotel on the island at the time. After several nights of luxury, especially enjoying the beautiful swimming pool (and the buffet breakfast), I ventured out by myself to find my *losmen* in Kuta. My package deal included a motorbike. Within days I had learnt to ride ... well sort of. I fell off the bike and landed in a rice *padi* and then the bike landed on top of me. I still have the scar on my inside right calf from the hot exhaust pipe burn to remind me (as do a generation of young Australians who travelled to Bali on a then famous 'drive yourself to debt or fly yourself to Bali' Garuda Airways promotion: return airfares, *losmen*, transport, welcome drink, breakfast and motorcycle hire).

But more than this, when I recall that first great adventure, I remember the happy times on an uncrowded Kuta beach and balmy evenings at *Yanie's Restaurant* or meandering through the coconut groves that are now the concrete and glass and plastic megalopolis of Kuta-Legion-Seminyak. And I remember Poppies Lane and buying fresh lobster for $1. I also ate a mushroom omelette somewhere and became delirious and then sick and then worse. Fortunately, I was nursed back to health by a kind Balinese family from my *losmen*. My arms and legs were covered in sores from the poison. It was not a good look. I actually don't remember much about it. It was all a blur really. But what I do recall is that I saw shadow puppets and also experienced a funeral ceremony; well I think I did— but again, perhaps it was the omelette? And of course it was the 1970's. It was 'magic'.

When I regained consciousness I moved to Ubud and met people from all over the World. I visited the Monkey Forest and bought a beautiful traditional painting which is still hanging in my home.

Ubud has matured and grown much better than Kuta Beach. More people near the sea than up a tree I suppose. The ambiance of Ubud remains largely peaceful, tropical and welcoming and, without doubt, the variety and quality of the food has improved. (I actually bought a toasted cheese and tomato sandwich at *Murni's Warung* and sat outside on the bench and ate it in the sun on that first trip. I remember it was pretty good too.) And of course, these days, there are a variety of activities around Ubud—especially the *Elephant Safari Park* at Taro and of course the fabulous Bali Adventure Tour white water rafting on the upper reaches of the Ayung River.

And not a 'magic' mushroom omelette restaurant in sight!

Today Ubud is the ideal place for David and me to rest, recuperate and recharge from our work commitments—the climate is so lovely. The air is still clean and the vegetation is deep and green and lush. And I know that there are plenty of things to keep me occupied ... if I want to be occupied—like the *Blanco Gallery* and the shops and the market and *Casa Luna* in town and *Murni's Warung* near the old bridge.

After working closely with some of Australia's largest property investors, I believe that there is nothing more certain than change. While Ubud has undoubtedly altered, it has grown within its limits with new developments, especially along the riverbank. These amazing properties—hotel and private homes alike, do not seem to impose upon the lushness of the *padi* fields. Rather the contrary. They feel part of the landscape. This is much like the 'new' dining balconies at *Murni's Warung*, which seem to fit perfectly into the contours of the river gorge below. (And unlike some of my unreliable memories of Kuta, I do actually remember the old *Murni's Warung*.)

Jayne Ward studied teaching at Wollongong University before moving to Mackay in North Queensland where she managed Langford's Hotel until 1998. Since that time she has built a successful career as a realtor working for many of Australia's largest property development companies. Jayne travels extensively for leisure and adventure with her partner David—who a senior sub-editor for Australia's largest circulation daily newspaper.

There once was a Boy...

Victor and Tanya Korin

We first came to Bali almost thirty years ago. We visited *Murni's* restaurant frequently and enjoyed her engaging conversations, her lively personality, amazing stories and, of course, her delicious food. One day we came a bit earlier than usual. The lady working in the restaurant at the time told us that Murni was in her room, so we decided to go and see her. As we approached we could hear what could only be described as 'heavenly' music coming from inside. It was a lovely Balinese melody—sweet and pure. We opened the door and saw Murni, dancing. She looked so graceful and beautiful. It was visually intoxicating. It amazed us to see Murni dance with such elegance and skill. We had no idea of her ability or, in fact, her very personal ambition for perfection.

Murni's dancing reminded us of a story we once heard.

There once was a boy who lived in a small village in the mountains. He was a gifted dancer, one of the best, in fact, a prodigy. One day, a local man decided to take him to a dance master in the city. The master asked the boy to dance but the boy could not. The old teacher sent the boy away, slightly annoyed at having his time seemingly wasted.

As soon as the boy arrived back in his village he began to dance again, with amazing skill and beauty.

The village elders immediately brought the boy back. But just as before, the boy could not dance. At this point, the wise old master suspected that something was wrong, intuitively walked up to the boy, took him by the shoulders, spun him around and pointed him in the direction and vista of the sacred peak in the mountains close to his home village. Suddenly, the boy began to dance as beautifully as he had ever danced. This was because the boy could now position himself to the holy mountain and could see exactly where he was.

Like the boy in the story, the dance in that small private room in Ubud cannot be separated from the rich collage of our lives. The very private dance, that surprised and delighted and enchanted us all those years ago, has become one of our most vivid memories of Murni—a strong, passionate, smart, visionary and kind friend—but more than that, her enchanting dance has become an everlasting memory of Bali itself.

Victor and Tanya Korin moved to Melbourne from Odessa, in the former USSR, in the late 1970's. After a few exciting years of working in different places in different positions, Tanya completed a course in travel consultancy. She then worked in this field, while Victor operated an engineering business, which they both built up over twenty years. A decade ago, Tanya discovered a passion for sculpture and painting. Since this time, she has contributed her work to a number of exhibitions. And Victor? He is enjoying working with driftwood (and doing some very occasional consulting work in engineering).

Learning and Creating

Vinder Balbir

My life shares many parallels with Murni's. Both of us were children during the political and social turmoil that engulfed Indonesia and Malaysia in the 1960's; both of us were hard working and optimistic (if not naïve) young entrepreneurs in the 1970's, starting in the restaurant business from nothing—Murni in Ubud and me in Bangkok; equally, during the 1980's, we expanded our horizons—Murni started building holiday accommodation and opening shops and I got into television and public relations. (And from the 1990's we both became famous for our deserts— me for mango *kulfi* and Murni for her pecan pie).

So when Murni was last in Bangkok, I invited her to have dinner with me and talk about life and the old days and it turned into an interesting discussion:

Murni: Vinder, what is your philosophy of life?

Vinder Balbir: My philosophy of life is centered around creativeness and expression.

Murni: Where do you think this came from?

Vinder Balbir: I learnt this from my experience of business. Because of my Indian cultural background I wasn't able to express my creativity easily; but then my cooking and my business taught me that if I held back I wouldn't be able to re-create what was inside me. In expressing and creating I am giving people the best stories, the best food, giving people the best dining experience—the best of everything. If you give 100% in everything you do in life, and you don't hold back, you cannot go wrong.

Murni: And your background is Malaysian?

Vinder Balbir: Yes, I was born in Kuala Lumpur. I went to school in Malacca and I graduated at the age of sixteen; and then almost immediately, I was a young bride. My parents were killed in the 1969 riots when I was eleven years old. That was a terrible time in my life, but I have become successful and happy because of what I learnt after I was orphaned. I went to a convent school, you know. The Catholic nuns taught me the spiritual side of life but also how to cook. I was often sent to the kitchen for 'punishment'. Can you imagine? I learnt that the nuns always gave their best, gave their 100% in the preparation of food. In the restaurant business when you want to give 100% you need the best ingredients, the best techniques, the best service, the best atmosphere. Everything has to be in balance.

Murni: Without that experience of your early childhood and the convent, would things have turned out differently?

Because I've had a very similar life, very tough in the early days; but now, more and more, I believe that it was the dark times that taught me the most.

Vinder Balbir: Exactly. I have friends whose life has been the opposite of mine. They had a life that was a bed of roses, then and now. Their journey has been a comfortable one. But perhaps not such a fulfilling one. But not me, and not you. I think most successful people go through hard times. You know you're successful when you can sit down like this and have dinner and the business runs itself. Before, I thought that I had to do everything myself. When I started to trust and when I surrendered to this trust, I became successful.

Murni: And the nuns in Malacca, did they teach you about Malaysian food?

Vinder Balbir: No, Italian food. Isn't that funny? When I first came to Thailand, I started teaching cooking at home. I offered classes to make ends meet. I taught my eager students how to make pizza, blueberry cheesecake and lasagna. This is what I learnt from the nuns. Then, when I got married to my husband, Mr Balbir, because he would only eat Indian food, of course I got more into that. I never went to Indian cooking classes or anything like that. I depended on my creativeness. It's like an inner life that tells me when it's time to put in the chili powder or it's time to add salt or potatoes.

Murni: I'm just the same. Learning and experiencing and creating, and making an income at the same time.

Vinder Balbir: Yes, it's also about business instinct. How many great chefs open businesses and fail because they are not business people? They only know about creativeness. I am blessed. I have both. I'm so glad that first came creativeness and then I discovered my ability to run a successful business.

I see these together as a gift from God.

Murni: But you have had to work hard for it—like me.

Vinder Balbir: Yes. Not holding back in anything. It's like when I discovered that I could talk in front of people on television. Yes, hard work, but again for me everything is based on creativeness and expression. If I said: 'Oh, I'm afraid' or 'I don't think I'm good enough' or 'I don't think I can do it.' If I held myself back, I wouldn't be where I am today. As an orphaned child, as a teenager in the convent, in the early days of my first restaurant, I would not let my fears hold me back.

Murni: What makes a successful restaurant, Vinder?

Vinder Balbir: It's what I call 'the warming up'. When someone comes into one of my restaurants, they sit at a table and begin to experience the atmosphere. There is, as they say, 'a vibration'. They look at the crockery, the setting, the chairs, the tables, the food, the smells, the sounds, the service, the physical layout, the space. A good restaurant is not just about the food—it's the integration of experiences. It's like what you do at *Murni's Warung*. I'm not here all the time now but, in the past, there would be a long line of people who didn't really come for the food, they came for me. And at *Murni's Warung* I know they came for you. But now they come for the atmosphere. Now many of my customers don't even know that I'm the owner. I go around the tables and they say: 'Who are you?' And when they finish I say: 'Thank you for coming. Was everything to your liking?' and they look at me like I'm crazy. So you see everything has to be in balance.

Murni: Tell me about your three favourite dishes.

Vinder Balbir: As you know, I like Thai food and I like Italian food too. I don't like complicated food. The mind has to register what the taste buds are experiencing. Let's say you are accustomed to eating *nasi goreng* (fried rice) and you find that the dish you are used to is now made with spaghetti, the mind takes a while to register. I don't understand food that causes confusion. I like traditional food. I would go for *tom yum* and fried rice and chicken in basil leaves or something like that. For Italian, I would go for spaghetti or pizza.

Murni: And for Indian food?

Vinder Balbir: If you give me black dal, *chapatis*, tandoori fish, *vindaloo*, I can eat this every day... with some nice yellow saffron rice.

Murni: You've been to Bali, was that for your television program?

Vinder Balbir: Yes! And of course after that you and I became good friends. I began asking people I met: 'Have you been to *Murni's Warung*?' I felt so happy in Bali. It is so rich there and the thing that amazed me most was the Hindu influence. It is so deep. That surprised me and I just loved the food. And like the rest of my life, once I discovered Balinese cooking, there was just no holding me back.

Murni: This time we are having dinner at one of your restaurants in Bangkok. Next time I would be delighted to have you as my guest at *Murni's Warung* in Ubud.

Vinder Balbir: That's very kind! I am happy to accept—but with one small condition. I would like some of your pecan pie for desert.

Vinder Balbir is a successful television host (*What's Cooking with Mrs. Balbir*) and owner of *Mrs. Balbir's Indian Restaurants* in Bangkok. Her cuisine has been featured on the BBC, in the

New York Times and in *Lonely Planet*. As founder of her own cooking school, she has taught Indian cooking to some of the World's best-known celebrity chefs. Vinder is an inflight meal consultant to *Thai International Airlines* and trained the personal cook of musician Sting. www.mrsbalbirs.com.

Her Bali

Albert Heath

I met Murni in 1976 at her small roadside *Warung* where her restaurant now stands. A friendship was established that still exists today, thirty-seven years later. Murni would lead us on many wonderful, exhilarating nature walks in the hills and valleys around Ubud.

We were, of course, all much younger and fitter in those days.

As our connection grew, small groups of us would pile into her car and off we would go exploring Bali. Usually we would finish up in Candi Dasa for great food and lovely ocean views at *Pandan*—a simple restaurant with a wonderful menu. Excellent food was always part of any outing and Murni knew the best places to eat, no matter where we were in Bali.

Much of what I have experienced and learned of Bali and Balinese culture has been fostered by Murni's introduction to 'Her Bali'. I admire and respect her generosity of spirit, her warmth, her love of life and her grace and charm. I have watched her grow in stature and influence over the years as Bali has developed into a World-class tourist destination. She has a special place as a cultural Ambassador, for 'Her Bali'.

A most remarkable woman.

Albert Heath has had a rich and varied career in fields as diverse as owning a famous restaurant called *Nats* in Aireys Inlet, a catering company specialising in one particular cake and his own fashion label concentrating on unisex denim jeans. These days he has hung up his apron but keeps wearing the jeans and is enjoying selling hats in the Melbourne markets, seascape photography, a spot of character acting and, of course, visiting Bali. Photograph by Jonathan Copeland.

A Family Affair

Janet Stride

Murni is one of the most interesting, intriguing and vibrant personalities that I have had the privilege to call my friend over what is, now, more than a quarter of a century.

My first introduction to the lady many people call *the Ibu of Ubud* was when travelling with a friend. Both of us were living in Jakarta and, for a break from the capital, we would travel to Ubud and not only have dinner at *Murni's Warung* but would have snacks at her house. Especially memorable was an extraordinary pineapple upside down cake. Immediately Murni made me feel like an 'old friend'. That warmth has never changed over the countless precious occasions that we enjoyed each other's company.

Subsequent visits—and there were many of them—to *Murni's Houses*, provided many opportunities to not only enjoy Murni's hospitality and that of her staff, but, even more importantly, gave me the chance to accompany her on treks through the rice fields, climb mountains, and even to visit her childhood village.

Even though I felt 'in good shape', Murni was always moving faster—everywhere; but most importantly, she shared her knowledge of everything from rice planting rituals to temple ceremonies. We laughed a lot and there was a special joy in watching her chat with everyone, from the rice farmer to the important local official.

Dressed in proper ceremonial clothes, my visits often included ceremonies ranging from marriages and temple anniversaries, to the most auspicious cremations on the Balinese Hindu calendar. But the most impressive ritual relating to Murni was her own 'tooth-filing', which was never performed when she was a teenager—considered the more traditional age to undertake such. Along with adult family members who also had yet to have this essential ceremony performed, Murni set out to make this an amazing customary journey and to share this experience with me.

I was so very fortunate to stay at her *Houses* for a week to observe the many preparations. This included thousands of offerings (each of them had to be perfect). These required dozens of ladies to work together in the family compound from morning until night—in two different shifts. The ceremony itself was wonderfully colourful with a cast of many participants. Sitting amongst her friends and neighbours, I listened to the sound of the *gamelan*, and felt so privileged to be part of that day.

Over the years, many of my family members have travelled from the USA to Bali and each one has had a chance to stay at *Murni's Houses* and enjoy the hospitality of her compound and staff. No matter where else they visit on the island, each one says that there is nothing to compare to this special place. From my newly married niece, both sisters and a brother who brought all six of his daughters and their spouses, it has provided a shared experience that is still talked about and will continue to be for many years to come.

My wish is to continue to nurture this special friendship that endures despite all the recent changes that have turned Ubud from a rather sleepy village without twenty-four hour electricity to a busy, 'must visit' destination for people from all over the World. Thank you Murni, for enriching our lives and counting us not only as friends but as family too.

Janet Stride is originally from Chicago. She and her New York born husband Ron moved to Jakarta in 1985 and since then has been intimately involved in the arts and cultures of Southeast Asia—in particular Indonesia. She has enjoyed collecting artworks and antiques from the cities that were also home since then, including Hong Kong, Bangkok and Singapore where she and Ron are now based. The Museum Study Groups in these locations have played an important part of this adventure, including Janet and Ron leading personalised tours to Bhutan and Bali for organization members. Travel remains an important and exciting part of Janet and Ron's lives.

The Dream to be 'Murni'

François Brikké

Ibu Murni is one of the key pioneers of Ubud. But, not many people know what it takes to reach success, especially when you are a woman in a very traditional society. The story of her life is an amazing tale, full of will and passion, tears and dreams, determination and contradictions, that progressively made her become a legend. When I first met Ibu Murni in 2010 in her peaceful and green guesthouse, *Murni's Houses* in Ubud, I was struck by her gentle and warm welcome as well as by her keen interest in knowing who I was. Not surprisingly, Murni means 'Pure' in Balinese.

This interest went beyond the common ritual questions that all Balinese people ask wherever you are: 'Where are you going? Where do you come from?' Indeed, Ibu Murni has an admirable gift in making you feel more than a special guest; you gradually become a long-time friend, and possibly even a member of her family. Not necessarily of her direct family, but of a wider family as the Balinese Hindus conceive it, an all-inclusive vision of the community where everyone has his place, and where you are appreciated as you are.

Without doubt, Ibu Murni is a 'people person', and it is this drive that has contributed to raising her to 'legend' status in Ubud, which goes well beyond the walls of her *Warung, Houses* and of the numerous shops that she owns today or owned in the past. However, to be a 'people person' is not a simple task; it requires time, devotion, curiosity, passion, patience, intuition and certainly compassion too; in the case of Ibu Murni, it has also led her many times to go beyond established social norms, which is particularly daring for a woman born in a strict Balinese Hindu traditional society.

In many ways, Ibu Murni has been a pioneer, setting an example for others, including her own family, and paving the way forward to the economic boom of Ubud in the early Eighties and beyond. Everything that she has started has become mainstream, from the establishment of a local restaurant, to the creation of shops selling local textiles, Balinese antiquities, Indonesian tribal art and the building of a comfortable and cosy guesthouse adapted to the desires and tastes of Westerners. What makes the fabric of a legend? In the case of Ibu Murni, the admirable courage and perseverance of a poor young girl who managed to propel herself to another dimension of life; perhaps also her empathy towards others and capacity to draw sympathy and trust. But the true essence of her legend is linked to the continuous quest of her dream, and on how it has been able to overcome hardship. The dream to be 'Murni'.

François Brikké is an international expert in development, a humanist and a novelist. He currently lives in Sweden, after having spent several years in Jakarta and Bali, but also in Africa, Latin America and Europe. His worldwide experience both at Government and Community levels is complemented by his involvement in humanist activities with the *Artisans of Peace* and the *Association Teilhard de Chardin*. He published his first novel *One Way Ticket to Paradise* in 2006 and is currently writing another novel *Spirit of a Legend*, based on Murni's life.

In the Company of Friends

José in den Kleef

The year was 1974. Murni was selling batik from her small shop near the Old Dutch Bridge in Ubud. Every day, Pat, Murni's American husband, would wander down for lunch. Murni would make him a bowl of soup and some sandwiches—toasted cheese if I recall. And he would contentedly sit there—out front, enjoying them. Tourists would walk past on their way to or from the Tjampuhan Hotel and see Pat and ask Murni if they could have some too. I believe that this gave Murni the idea that she could make a few extra sandwiches and, as they say, earn a crust. And that's how *Murni's Warung* started.

From 1981 until 1994, my husband Ron and I, together with some other Dutch people, owned a small hotel in Kedewatan-Ubud. It was called *Cahaya Dewata*. It was a lovely place with a magnificent view and, at that time, it was in the middle of nowhere.

When the hotel was quiet, we would walk the three kilometres down to *Murni's Warung* to have lunch or dinner. Indeed, we actually walked, usually in the middle of the road, as at that time there were hardly any cars on the road and—unbelievable as it now seems—no motor-cycles. I have to admit, the way back home involved more climbing than the way down but Ron and I always felt it was worth the effort. What pleased us most, however, was not the good food but the chance to meet such a friendly hostess; Murni seemed to be always present, talking with guests, listening to their stories and giving tips on how best to explore Bali. Everyone felt welcome and special. And so Murni and I became friends.

It was around this time that 'The House' was built. This was to be the first building of what is now *Murni's Houses* in Campuhan-Ubud. In those days, Murni would come to meet us at *Cahaya Dewata* and, in turn, we had the pleasure to be invited to her new home.

My husband Ron passed away in 1996 and the hotel was sold. To be truthful, this was a terrible time for me; still, I decided to continue my visits to Bali. My deep connection with Ubud and my wonderfully supportive old *Cahaya Dewata* friends and my friendship with Murni all proved to play an important role in overcoming part of my grief.

Since this time, I have stayed at *Murni's Houses* twice a year; each visit for about a month; and so I naturally became a daily guest at *Murni's Warung*. I have to admit, I seldom have dinner in the restaurant part of the *Warung*, but I frequently visit the Lounge Bar with its charming ambiance and enjoy the reliable and excellent company. I always eat there. And so I have spent many pleasant hours in that lounge and I was (and still am) very glad to be taken home by the free taxi-shuttle. Sure, the distance between *Murni's Houses* and *Murni's Warung* is not far—'as the crow flies'—but for my over 80-

year old legs it is becoming a bit of a challenge to navigate the steep ascent.

No story about Murni and about *Murni's Warung* would be complete without mentioning the staff who always make me feel welcome in *Murni's Houses*, in the restaurant and in the Lounge Bar. If they were not there, business would not be possible. They always take such good care of me and are ceaselessly friendly, kind and helpful. Yes, they are doing their 'job' but in my view, appreciation for the good work of Murni's wonderful staff is more important than merely benefiting from it or accepting it.

For forty wonderful years, *Murni's Warung* has been, and always will be, somewhere to enjoy life, experience excellent service, eat good food and relish the company of friends.

José in den Kleef was born in southeastern Holland, close to both the Belgian and German borders. Now in her eighth decade, she was an educator her entire working life—first teaching French and English and later Pedagogics in a Teachers' Training College. José's husband Ron was born in the old colonial *Nederlands Oost Indie* before World War II. In 1949, he had to leave Indonesia but often said that he left the greater part of his heart behind. Ron and José returned to Indonesia many times over the years. After Ron passed away, José continued to visit Bali—her 'second home'.

Murni's Warung

Dr. Lawrence Blair

I'd already been shooting TV documentaries in remote parts of Indonesia for several years with my late brother, Lorne, before managing to reach Bali. Some of my earliest memories of the island are entwined with long and happy hours spent at *Murni's Warung,* which was Ubud's sole nexus of cross-cultural communication. Although Lorne had already reached Bali with our adventurous mother a year beforehand, I arrived a few months before *Murni's Warung* first opened in 1974.

I'd flown in from Los Angeles and arrived at the airport when, as some may remember, you could pick frangipani blossoms off the trees before you entered the tiny immigration and customs terminal. It was night and I decided to rent a motorbike, shoulder my backpack and make my way up to Ubud to find my family. It was an impulsive move, as there was no moon and no signposting at all on the roads, except for one, just north of Denpasar, saying TO UBUD. As I ascended higher into the hills on a road with numerous deceptive forks, the villages were already in darkness and there was no one on the roads to ask directions from. But vague thoughts of having to spend the night in a paddy field dissolved as the starry sky and the scents of the surrounding jungle completely enveloped me. And then, the fireflies! Multitudes of them, all around me and high up in the trees. I no longer cared about anything and, as is the way of things when one no longer cares, I unerringly found my way to my goal, the tiny *losmen* where my family was staying in Ubud.

Ubud and its satellite villages were truly exotic in the 1970's: inexhaustibly cheerful communities tending their rice paddies, fruit orchards and temples, while still having time to knock off endless imaginative paintings and carvings. No phones, electricity, taxis or fresh milk or butter. But these inconveniences paled against an environment where we could take long bare-footed walks through 'Shakespearean hedgerows', swim in concealed streams and natural pools and experience full moon nights in the then still separate and forbidding monkey forest.

Instead of tourists, there were only a few 'travellers' and barely a handful of eccentric resident expats. And the place to meet them was *Murni's Warung*. But the first real draw to *Murni's* was the discovery that hers was the sole place in Ubud to have mastered that most rare and esoteric art of producing a sunny-side up properly fried egg.

Further cause for enthusiasm was when she also became the first person in Ubud to provide natural yoghurt and wild honey with one's tropical fruit.

Murni more than earned her common soubriquet of Ibu—for she was everyone's mother, in its broadest sense. Not only was she a great publican but she also pioneered selling exotic merchandise from beyond Bali: batik *sarongs* which she'd brought back from Java, woven *ikat* from Sumba and Savu and some of the first of those beautiful woven rattan baskets from Borneo. This was also a gathering place for both foreign and domestic traders of Indonesian ethnographic art and textiles, where we could hear those inventive word symphonies surrounding their values and origins.

Amongst the many lesser and better known people I either took to or met at *Murni's* were scores of intriguing travelers from Goa, Tibet, New York and Argentina, as well as Richard Branson, Mick Jagger, Richard Gere, Diane Von Furstenberg, the American guru Ram Das (formerly Richard Alpert) and the artist Abdul Mati Klarwein, to name but a few. My only regret is that they weren't all there at the same time.

Ibu Murni had indeed chosen the perfect spot, just where the antique and abandoned steel Dutch bridge crossed the River Wos. A new bridge, just a few yards to the eastward, had already been built but was still so narrow in the 1970's that there wasn't room for vehicles to cross in both directions at the same time. So, sitting in *Murni's Warung* at street level provided a constantly entertaining theatre of the infancy of traffic etiquette, which has since evolved into the clearer principle that the biggest wins.

I have a memory of *Murni's Warung*, which I must share, less for its ability to enlighten others than for its purgative value on my own psyche.

It was not unfashionable to wear exotic clothes, and often very few of them. I happened to be wearing only a pair of those loose, tie-around Vietnamese farmers' trousers of light cotton and no shirt. I left the restaurant one morning, still full of customers, and mounted my rather handsome motorbike parked right out front. I kick-started the bike with a satisfying roar but only advanced half a metre because my trousers had been instantly torn off and wrapped round the back axel, leaving me entirely naked, unable to either restart the bike and drive off or even to push it out of view—though I made an effort at both of these manoeuvers, to the raucous delight of the patrons. All I could do was to stride back into the *Warung* as blithely as possible and ask Murni if she could sell me a *sarong*, fairly soon. She obliged me with an entirely straight face.

Thank you, Murni, for being around so lovingly and for so long, in this illusory land where so little seems constant.

Dr. Lawrence Blair is an anthropologist, author and film-maker who has been based in Bali and exploring Indonesia for nearly forty years. With his late brother, Lorne, he is the co-producer of the BBC and PBS adventure series on Indonesia called *Ring of Fire*, winner of 2 Emmy Awards in 1988. His recent TV films include *Myths, Magic and Monsters* and *Bali—Island of Dogs*.

Our Second Home

Colette Ghysels

I suppose what first brought us to Bali is that we had friends living there. To say they 'exhorted' us to come is something of an understatement. So, because we love travelling and because our friends insisted, in 1980 we journeyed across the planet to the little island Nehru called *The Morning of the World*.

Jean-Pierre, having won a major sculpture prize in the form of a travelling grant, drove a *Citroën 2CV* from Belgium to India where I had a reunion with him in Delhi. I arrived from Africa, where I was working for an international organisation. As Nepal was opening its borders, we decided to drive there and got married in Kathmandu on 27 December 1959. It was a time when no one knew Kathmandu, except for some alpinists, of course, and the Tibetans fleeing the Chinese invasion. The legendary *2CV* became our first home!

One of the things that have brought us back to Bali every year is that we are collectors of ethnic jewelry. When in Bali, I always get in touch with Murni. She has a great collection herself and, on one of her early trips to Europe in the mid-1980s, she visited me in Brussels. Seven books have already been published about our collection—the first in 1994 was *Splendor of Ethnic Jewelry*, published by Harry N. Abrams, and from 2000-2005, a thematic series *A World of (1) Rings (2) Earrings (3) Bracelets (4) Necklaces (5) Belts and (6) Head Ornaments*, published by Skira. We have also contributed to an exhibition at the Wereld Museum in Rotterdam called *The Magic of Women* where we were the major lender. The theme was Indonesian women's textiles and jewelry. It was a wonderful show in a wonderful museum. Murni would have loved it.

Going back to the early days, for us, Indonesia was a new sphere of collecting and, of course, there were the wonderful Indonesian textiles we discovered. Murni was (and still is) someone who has greatly helped us in that field. What struck us most in Bali, and influenced our lives both consciously and I suppose even sub-consciously, is the Balinese people's tolerance towards visitors and foreign cultures. We have always been amazed by this and at times resentful (is that the right word?) towards some Western people who regrettably do not respect this rich and wonderful culture. The consequences have been the Balinese forbidding foreigners to attend some religious ceremonies at *Besakih* (the Mother Temple)—a privilege I am pleased to say we have experienced ourselves.

If that miraculous little *2CV* was our 'first home', then Bali has become our extraordinary 'second home'. As I said, we have been to Bali at least once a year since that first visit all those years ago—and it seems that Murni has always been part of this wonderful adventure. In fact, we think of Murni as a 'legend'—but unlike legends in which there are witches and monsters, for us, Murni is a fairy godmother!

Bali is like Murni; she is mesmerizing. Each year I momentarily wonder why is it that we return to that *Island of Gods and Demons* instead of going to other wonderful and loved places we have never been to? But then I remember that it is partly because there is not a Murni everywhere else. Although we do not see her each time we visit—as like us, Murni is often travelling—one has a sense that, in case of need, it will always be possible to reach her and get help or advice: these are my feelings for Murni.

She is loved by everyone, poor or rich, and she is completely herself with everyone. Murni is no doubt a woman of her time but wonderfully attached to her culture and her community. I admire her for working in her *Warung* and shops, not just for herself but for her entire community, creating opportunity and employment, attending and preparing for ceremonies and offerings, even returning from abroad to attend an important religious event. Our hope is that the Gods will bless her and everything she does.

For me, Murni is the perfect example of what can be achieved by determination and hard work. She is known all over the World for her deep sense of ethics and for the unceasing care she extends to all. I know that her own background is, in her own words, 'humble' and she has not forgotten how she started in life. I am not surprised that, like the island of Bali itself, Murni is a magnet for so many travellers; but more than that she has the warmth of a mother, the most beautiful smile and an unforgettable twinkle in her eyes.

Colette Ghysels was born in Cairo of an Armenian mother and a Belgian father, both great travellers, who introduced her to the world of carpets, textiles and ethnic jewelry on the one side and primitive arts on the other. Her first piece of ethnic jewelry was given to her—at her own request—for her 14th birthday and, since then, she has only worn genuine ethnic pieces. Colette and her husband Jean-Pierre have compiled one of the World's finest private collections of ethnic jewelry which, until recently, has remained carefully protected in Brussels, never exhibited extensively and accessible only to selected scholars. Several publications showcase a fraction of her life's passion: *Splendor of Ethnic Jewelry: From the Colette and Jean-Pierre Ghysels Collection, A World of Belts, A World of Bracelets, A World of Earrings, A World of Head Ornaments, A World of Necklaces* and *A World of Rings* which bring to light the Ghysels Collection in glorious photographs. In *Splendor of Ethnic Jewelry*, Colette Ghysels herself provides detailed captions for all the illustrations. Other major exhibitions of the Colette and Jean-Pierre Ghysels collection include the *Palazzo Reale* in Milan, *the Palazzo Strozzi* in Florence, *Speyer Museum* (Germany), the *Museum of Asian Arts* in Nice, the *Baur Foundation* in Geneva and the *Jacques Chirac Museum* (France).

Princess Lala
(Murni) McTavish

David Raitt

My Dad, the late John Raitt, was a main force during the golden age of American musical theatre. He is best known for his lead stage roles in *Carousel*, *Oklahoma!*, *The Pyjama Game*, *Carnival in Flanders*, *Three Wishes for Jamie*, *A Joyful Noise* and *Annie Get Your Gun* with Mary Martin. He also performed throughout the US in *South Pacific* and had a hit song in his day with *Some Enchanted Evening*. (And of course I remember *Bali Ha'i*).

Dad enjoyed seeing everything good on stage in New York in those days. My earliest memory of Bali was my father telling me about the Lady Bumblebee Balinese dance performance at the

Fulton Theatre in New York City in the 1950's. But, like most Americans of my generation, my fascination with this faraway exotic place was based, I suppose, more on seeing the Bing Crosby and Bob Hope film *Road to Bali*—which actually had practically nothing to do with Bali except that I was convinced that it did and that Dorothy Lamour really was Princess Lala McTavish.

I have been to Bali three times. The highlight of one trip was a long lunch hosted by Murni herself on the veranda of her home. It was so generous. I felt like Harold Gridley (Bob Hope) in a scene from the movie singing (not dancing) and playing guitar after the banquet—which miraculously appeared, course by course by course through a hatch in the wall, as Princess Lala McTavish, sorry, Murni, kept my Californian companions mesmerized with wonderful stories about Ubud 'in the old times', and about her travels and adventures. And, between the main course and dessert of fresh fruit and homemade yogurt with local honey, Murni showed us her Aladdin's cave of antiques and textiles and traditional musical instruments. I recorded a piece on my Garage Band iPhone application using several ancient Balinese xylophones and imagined how cool it would sound as a blues fusion. And then, between dessert and coffee, we all trekked down the side of the hill, traversing the rice *padi* to where two rivers join and refreshed ourselves in the holy water that poured out of a stone-carved monster head. For one magical afternoon time stood still—and, before we knew it, the sun was setting over the terraced river valley below and it was time to prepare for dinner—at *Murni's Warung*. I felt like king of the World.

Many Americans are nervous about Indonesia—and most other places for that matter—but not Ubud, which really is an international cultural capital. There is something about Ubud; and if you ever get the chance to spend a lazy afternoon with Murni, I think you'll discover what I mean.

Bali Ha'i may call you, Any night, any day

David Raitt is a yurt designer, building contractor and yurt dweller who has built yurts and trained 'yurters' on five continents over three decades. David splits his time between California and Pescadero, in the lower Baja, Mexico, where he writes and records music in his studio. David Raitt and Jimmy Thackery celebrated their thirty-year reunion by recording the critically acclaimed album *That's It* in 2000. This album featured horn work by Mic Gillette of *Tower of Power* fame as well as vocal additions by Bonnie Raitt. These days David is spending more time touring with *The Baja Boogie Band*. See him on You Tube: www.youtube.com/watch?v=qgghwOCCHkg. Photograph by Chek Wingo.

The Human Travel Guide

Betty Hintz

I actually didn't meet Murni until 1989, although I had been visiting my adored Bali since 1968. It took a total of nine journeys there, and a recommendation from daughter Tina, to get me to the *Warung*; and eventually I introduced myself. *Murni's Warung* and *Murni's Warung Shop* are very Balinese, but I believe it is nice for those tourists not as enamoured of Indonesian food as I to be able to get a hamburger or carrot cake at her wonderful restaurant. And, yes, the setting is amazing. It must have been an engineering feat to build the multi-leveled edifice overlooking the gorge. What genius! Actually, when my family first visited Ubud it was mostly rice fields. We had been driven over the old bridge and taken by the driver to Antonio Blanco's studio.

On a subsequent visit to Han Snel's studio I purchased a sketch he had done of his wife Siti. It hangs over my fireplace and probably shocks my more staid friends, as she is bare breasted. I can think of nothing on earth more tranquil than sitting on the veranda of the Bungalow at *Murni's Houses*, her accommodation, after a day's sightseeing, cool drink in hand, watching the bats (which come out in the late afternoon) swirling about after the multitudes of dragonflies.

The breeze is always cool and the setting is idyllic. For me, Murni is a human travel guide; she knows just what is going on and where—and then she either takes you there herself or directs your driver. Unusual ceremonies may be witnessed, colourful parades viewed, religious rites seen. I don't think I have ever known a more giving human being than our beautiful Murni. It certainly was a blessed occasion the day I met her.

Betty Hintz has spent a lifetime travelling and living in nearly every country in Southeast Asia. She first visited Bali in the 1960's—even before *Murni's Warung* was a conception. Since then she's been many times and is planning her 90th birthday celebrations at *Murni's Warung*. She retired recently from managing a well-known Scottish company for which she did the buying and spends her spare time teaching a diverse range of subjects on Southeast Asian Studies at the University of South Carolina.

Reflections on Ibu Murni

Peter O'Neill

The last thing I did on my first visit to Ubud in November 1980 was to have a meal at *Murni's Warung*. As I recall, it was late one weekday night. I'd spent the previous few days taking *genggong* lessons from Bapak (Mr) Togog in Peliatan, meeting the painter Antonio Blanco, of whom I'd heard so much about, and wandering the streets and surrounding fields of what I'd come to feel was one of the most remarkable places on the planet. (The *genggong* is a bamboo jaw harp found in Bali, Indonesia. It usually is played in pairs with one instrument slightly larger than the other with a corresponding higher pitch.)

I'd been told about *Murni's Warung*, how it sat perched atop a sharp ravine and meandered floor by floor down ever closer to waters that gushed in rapturous applause to a menu that would both excite and educate. Some friends of mine had urged me to check it out but I'd thought that their descriptions must have been wildly exaggerated. I wish I hadn't ignored their advice until the last moment because I would have eaten there far more often in my first four-day stay.

Those wildly exaggerated claims in fact turned out to be understatements. It wasn't until over twenty years had passed that I met Ibu Murni herself and had the opportunity to discover the person whom I had come to regard as 'The Queen of Ubud'. I had made infrequent trips to Bali over those years but now I had a reason to seek her out. I was involved in an exhibition of textile and fibre-based works by Australian artists that was to become Australia's first contribution to the *Bali Arts Festival*, Asia's oldest continuous cultural festival. One contact after another led me to *Murni's Villas*, her extraordinarily rich private collection and her perfect blend of gracious urbanity and Balinese charm.

The exhibition project had grown out of all proportion and we needed to find suitable accommodation for some Australian dignitaries who were to attend the festival opening and other events where they were to be presented to the President of the Republic of Indonesia as well as governors, *bupatis*, ambassadors, government ministers and local dignitaries. After being presented to the President and the Governor of Bali and dining with regents and *bupatis*, *Murni's Villas* provided an oasis after four days of intense and unforgettable cultural and social experiences.

One such experience was attending the playoffs of the two finalists in the annual competition between *gamelans* from over forty sub-districts of Bali. More like *Iron Chef* than *My Kitchen Rules*, the two *gamelans* sat opposite each other on the stage and belted out piece after piece, occasionally overlaid by hoots or hollers from the audience as one *gamelan* out-shone or out-performed their opponent at critical moments and progressed towards the highly charged finale.

Over the next decade, there were many reasons for me to return to Ubud, however the most memorable occurred after another cultural project, this time based in the Central Javanese Sultanate of Yogyakarta. This opportunity enabled me to bring my eight-year old son Julian to Bali for the first time. Of course we stayed at *Murni's Villas* to recuperate after two weeks of exhibition installation and attending events. The excitement, stress and sheer physical hard work of our time in Yogyakarta seemed to instantly dissolve the moment my son and I hit *Murni's Villas'* extraordinary infinity pool. Later that evening my wide-eyed son Julian and I were leisurely considering the menu at *Murni's Warung* when Murni herself appeared, and with her characteristic warmth and charm again recommended that I order one of her signature dishes—called *Murni's Fish*—sautéed tengiri served with vegetables and a special sauce. This was rounded off with Black Rice Pudding and fresh coconut milk—still made fresh from scratch every day. In fact, as it turned out, this was the very same meal combination I ordered on that first night of sheer dining delight all those years ago in late November 1980.

Peter O'Neill, OAM, is an arts administrator with over forty years' experience in the development, management and leadership of art museums and representative organisations within the arts and cultural sector. His first contact with Indonesian culture came through playing Javanese *gamelan* at the University of Western Australia in the late 1970's and early 1980's. He has since worked on cultural and people-to-people exchanges between Australia and Indonesia and is currently a principal consultant with Cultural Consulting. www.culturalconsulting.com.au.

My Friend and my Light

Laura Rosenberg
(back row, fourth from the right)

I met Ni Wayan Murni on my first trip to Bali—
with John Coast—in 1983. She came to see us in
Sayan where my friend Jenny Vogel and I were
staying with James Murdoch. (There was only one
house there then and no *Four Seasons Hotel* to spoil
one of the most beautiful views in Bali.) When John
arrived I stayed with him at the nearby rebuilt Colin
McPhee home. We both loved Murni immediately.
John and I saw her again in London a few years
later where we were living and working—John
had his own artists' management business and I
worked for another company (mostly managing
conductors and instrumentalists).

The story of how John Coast brought a
Balinese dance troupe to Europe and the United
States in 1952-53 with the support of President
Sukarno to honor Indonesia's independence in an

East-West cultural event is well known. His celebrated book *Dancing Out of Bali* chronicles how he revived the Peliatan dance troupe—including introducing Raka, the gifted twelve-year old Balinese *legong* dancer, to the world—and how the group performed for a global theatre audience of over 30 million people (including a live performance on the Ed Sullivan television show). I had arranged for Periplus, the leading publisher in Indonesia, to reprint *Dancing Out of Bali* to coincide with the 50th anniversary of the British edition in 2004. Sir David Attenborough, (who worked with John on a BBC documentary about Bali twenty years before John's death in 1989) wrote the brilliant foreword. The book featured recently researched photographs with detailed captions. It was relaunched at the *ARMA Foundation* (*Agung Rai Museum of Art* in Ubud, a center for visual and performing arts) in late 2004 where we showed the kinescope of the 1952 television performance of *Oleg Tumulilingan*, a dance commissioned for the tour by John Coast from the famous Balinese choreographer Mario and shown on American television. This dance is performed in Bali to this day. What deserves retelling here is the story of a remarkable private reunion dinner and what this says about Murni's generosity, compassion and sensitivity—as well as her support and friendship for me personally.

The night after the official launch, Murni invited about thirty guests to her *Warung* and we had a private feast of Balinese specialities. It was a very touching thing for her to do and a great memory for all of those present. Raka, as well as Anom and Oka (the two other *legong* dancers), were there. It was a fantastic reunion for them—and the last time all three would be together. The spellbinding drummer, Anak Agung Gedé Ngurah Mandera, who led the *gamelan* orchestra on the tour, was represented by his son Agung Bagus, who like his father is a very handsome and talented *gamelan* dancer and musician. And dear James Murdoch, the Australian musicologist came with his old friend, the renowned Malaysian dancer Ramli Ibrahim—and James made a wonderful and passionate speech.

I am so grateful to Murni for organizing and presiding over such a wonderful evening. It was the happiest of reunions and reaffirmation of old friendships. It was a perfect collision of timing, and circumstance, and characters. That night will live in my memory like the flame from a bright candle. For that wonderful night at *Murni's Warung*, and for so very much more, Murni will always be the best sort of friend—one who balances me with her strength and inner peace and whose generosity is overwhelming.

Laura Rosenberg was John Coast's companion for the last fifteen years of his life. She established the *John Coast Foundation for the Performing Arts in Bali* and remains in close contact with the living members of the Peliatan *gamelan* as well as the family of Anak Agung Mandera. She lives in New York City in an apartment with many objects and textiles chosen with exquisite taste by Murni. She cohabits with a cockatiel, two dogs and her husband, the radio humorist, Steve Post. Photograph by Jonathan Copeland.

Dreaming and Waking

Prairie Prince

Bali was somewhere I had always wanted to visit ever since I can remember. Some friends had been in the 1970's and returned with blissful tales of this far off magical land—rich in culture—in particular art and music—for me a true paradise. For decades, I had a vivid and reoccurring dream of a place that I eventually discovered was, in fact, Bali. My dream may have been, in part, inspired by the fact that my sister Helen Prince had been to the island with our dear friend Barbara Golden and our niece Francesca Raimond in the late 1990's to participate in a *Bali Arts Festival* musical performance by *Sekar Gaya*—a *gamelan* orchestra from Berkeley California. Helen produced a documentary film that chronicled the events surrounding the group's concerts and their interactions with other Balinese and American musicians (http://taksu-bali-doc.com).

A few years later, Barbara and Helen organized another festival performance—only this time, it included me. It was a piece especially composed for a mixed ensemble. We stayed in a small hotel called *Dewi Sri* and rehearsed at the *Çudamani School* and a nearby temple. This was the ultimate experience for a first time visitor—especially a musician. I relished the company of my new friends and was consumed with the kaleidoscope of rich and colourful experiences; and this included lunch at *Murni's Warung*. I recall how I was taken with the beauty and elegance of the architecture and décor, not to mention the fabulous food, excellent service and warm hospitality. More than a few years passed until, in 2005, I woke from a dream and Bali again called me. We rented a villa called *Taman Otto* in the village of Bedulu near the Elephant Cave. We stayed for six glorious weeks taking in the atmosphere, playing Balinese music and meeting more Balinese musicians.

Murni's Warung was a favorite place to eat—many times; still I didn't get the opportunity to meet her. Finally, in 2010, the next adventure began and we rented the villa in Bedulu for a second time, with friends Jason Wood and Mark Sadeghian, who had told us of their recent stay at *Murni's Villas* and what an incredible time they had. They arranged a lunch for all of us at Murni's private home where we finally found Murni and her friend and partner Jonathan who treated us with kind-hearted affection and the most wonderful hospitality. It was as if we had been friends for years—and, I suppose indirectly, we had been. We dined on breadfruit and a new drink concoction of Murni's making consisting of beets, lime and cream at a banquet table overlooking rice terraces.

The grounds at *Murni's Villas* were spectacular and we were given the tour with an anything goes flare. The infinity pool was exceedingly inviting and we luxuriated in the calm waters with the sounds of the jungle all around us. It was, in a word, 'blissful', even 'gleeful' (but that's two words—three if you count 'even'—but, then again, I'm a drummer). And, of course, as I write this contribution to the 40th anniversary of *Murni's Warung*, I am planning my next trip. I have been having those dreams again—Bali is calling.

Prairie Prince was raised in Phoenix, Arizona, with two older sisters who lavished constant musical influences upon him, including swing, jazz, blues and early rock and roll. Both of his parents were music lovers and his father played drums. His mother was an artist. Prairie moved to San Francisco to take up a scholarship at the *San Francisco Art Institute*. In 1976, Mr Hagiwara introduced Prairie to his new Yamaha drums, which he has endorsed and played with pride ever since. Prairie has worked with many of the World's most celebrated musicians including Nicky Hopkins, George Harrison, Mick Taylor, Ron Wood, Ray Cooper, Klas Voorman, Tommy Bolin, Brewer and Shipley, Chris Isaak, Brian Eno and David Byrne. Over the last few years he has concentrated on studio work with renowned producer Jerry Harrison of *Talking Heads* fame (who has also stayed at *Murni's Villas*), contributing to records by Bizou Phillips and Noella Hutton, both young innovative female artists, as well as performances on a double/live CD with *Grateful Dead* Bassist Phil Lesh, and a CD with long-time friend and former *Tubes* and *Grateful Dead* member, Vince Welnick (*Missing Man Formation*), which brought wide acclaim from a unique base of music fans. See him on You Tube: www. youtube.com/watch?v=Ts36vw8Gev8.

Remembrances of Murni's Comfort Zone

Dr. Lisa Gold

As a central gathering place of multicultural friendship, it is fitting that *Murni's Warung*, perched on the edge of a lush, green ravine, hovers over the meeting of two rivers in Campuhan. The calming sound of the rushing water, birds singing and insects humming permeate the atmosphere the moment you step into this cool bamboo structure, open to Bali's natural sounds and sights. This is the Bali of everyone's expectations and dreams, steeped in the history of ethnographic writings of those who lived nearby in an earlier era. We now know that these writers romanticized Bali and that Balinese life cannot be contained in these crystallized images of paradise. Bali is a vibrant, actively changing, modern, global society that has always been open to influences from the outside world. Yet, somehow, stepping into *Murni's Warung* allows us a space and time to suspend critical enquiry, temporarily, and to simply enjoy certain aspects of Bali that are also very real.

When I first arrived in Bali in 1981, I had already been studying *gamelan* (Balinese ensemble music) and *wayang kulit* (shadow puppetry) for several years in California.

After finishing my BA in Music at UCLA and many years of *gamelan* immersion with some of Bali and Java's finest performers in residence in the US, and playing in *Gamelan Sekar Jaya* in Berkeley, I accompanied my friends Michael Tenzer and Rachel Cooper to live in the village of Peliatan at Pak Ketut Madra's Homestay where I stayed for thirteen months.

There was no electricity in most of Peliatan and Ubud then. I lived in the village and spent most of my time in other, more remote villages, studying and spending time with the families of my teachers, eating whatever food they could offer, such as eels from the *sawah* and rice. Occasionally I would treat myself to a trip up to Campuhan to *Murni's*. My friend Michael Tenzer introduced me to Ibu Murni when I first arrived in Bali and I always felt so special when I walked in and was greeted with her warm, friendly charm and delicious food.

I remember Ibu Murni telling me again and again that she was so pleased that I, as a woman, was playing *gamelan*, an art form that she herself had wished she could have studied as a girl. At that time *gamelan* playing was restricted to males, so when I joined the first female group in Denpasar (*Gamelan Puspa Sari*) led by Ketut Suryathini and Wayan Suweca, (and we performed on *TVRI*) I was part of a landmark event that opened the way for many little girls and women to become musicians. The image of Murni's excitement and enthusiasm about my *gamelan* playing will always stay with me and, added to my desire to encourage the girls and women in our first women's *gamelan* ensemble to take it seriously. There was something so personal about the *Warung* at that time, with its carefully made yogurt and muesli and soups and other delicacies that made me feel at home in Bali. When I had a birthday, Murni made me a whole banana cake, decorated with woven palm leaf ornaments and flowers. I was very moved by this. I was living on a very tight budget that year— trying to extend the little money I had as long as possible, so going up to Ubud to *Murni's Warung* was a big splurge for me at the time. When I needed some home comfort or a special treat, I would take the *bemo* up and walk in and be treated like an important family friend.

I always felt I was momentarily stepping outside of the village life of my teachers to one more familiar to me in certain ways, where I could just eat potato soup, grilled cheese sandwiches and chocolate cake quietly. At that time, there were no other places to get this kind of food, which must be hard to imagine for those visiting Ubud today! Murni was always so comfortable in both worlds, as a strong, independent Balinese woman. Since that time, I have been immersed in the world of *gamelan* and *wayang*, as a performer and scholar. When I lived in Bali in 1992-93 with my husband and one-year old son, doing my Ph.D. dissertation research, I began to experience Bali through the eyes of a parent. We would bring our son to *Murni's* where people working there would all want to hold him and show him things—an image that is very clear in my mind.

My intensely close relationships with my music teachers brought me deeply into other worlds: the *wayang* world of characters, stories, philosophy, history, magic, humor, and the Balinese present. My teachers would share with me memories of *zaman dulu*—a bygone past in which the *wayang* was more central in people's lives, full of rich materials no longer in use by the 1980's, yet remaining in the minds of performers as cognitive maps that informed their current experience. This body of knowledge was so powerful to them it became the central thread of my dissertation on *gender wayang* in

Bali (to become a book). Many of those performers are now deceased and I have been focusing on *wayang* and *gender wayang* performance of the younger generations, looking at connections among a complex transmission network of players through time and space. I compare the vibrant performance scene today in which numerous Balinese children—including girls—are engaged in *gamelan, wayang,* dance, and theater performance, with the body of knowledge of my earlier teachers who were immersed in their ideas of *zaman dulu*. But I too have images of my *zaman dulu,* when I first lived in Bali, and *Murni's Warung* plays a part in that. I am thankful to be able to revisit that past every time I walk through the door.

Dr. Lisa Gold (Ph.D. in Ethnomusicology from UC Berkeley) has performed *gender wayang* and Balinese and Javanese *gamelan* and conducted research extensively in Bali and the US, and is the author of the book *Music in Bali: Experiencing Music, Expressing Culture* in the Oxford University Press Global Music Series (2005), and *The Gender Wayang Repertoire in Theater and Ritual* (Ph.D. Dissertation, University of California at Berkeley, 1998). Her research interests include Balinese and Javanese music in ritual and theater, *gamelan gender wayang,* shadow puppetry, folklore and folk music of the British Isles, oral performance and improvisation, sound studies, music, place and spatial orientation and transmission and performance eco-systems. She is a member of *Gamelan Sekar Jaya, Gamelan Sari Raras,* and *Shadow Light*. Lisa teaches at the University of California at Berkeley, assists in the Balinese *gamelan* program there, and has taught at *Colorado College, San Francisco Conservatory of Music, Mills College,* and *California State University San Jose*. She is very thankful to have studied and worked with some of Bali and Java's finest performers, including I Wayan Loceng, I Made Lebah, I Nyoman Rajeg, Nyoman Sumandhi, I Wayan Suweca, I Wayan Nartha, I Wayan Wija, I Made Subandi, K.R.T. Wasitodiningrat, I.M. Harjito and Midiyanto.

The Ancestors will be Delighted

Paola Gianturco

Galungan, the holiday that welcomes ancestral spirits to earth for a ten-day visit, is two days away. In the Ubud market there are vendors with baskets of hibiscus, frangipani blossoms and edible offering ingredients: hard-boiled eggs, fruit, cookies colored with neon pink food dye. All offering materials come from the earth (flowers, leaves, fruit, grain, and fowl) and will be transformed by cooking, cutting, mixing and assembling to please the ancestors' sense of taste, smell and beauty. In Bali, opposites are believed to derive meaning from their complements. Black represents the feminine, red the masculine; black, red and white symbolize the unity of the universe and the creation of life.

Not surprisingly, men and women play distinct, complementary roles in holiday preparations. For *Galungan*, men construct bamboo altars and *penjors* (arches) in front of every house. Women decorate the *penjors* and altars, plus create offerings to be blessed at the temple. As a young woman in the 1960's, Ni Wayan Murni was the first vendor to sell *sarongs* on the beach when Australian and American hippies discovered Bali. She used her proceeds to open *Murni's Warung* in Ubud, now a popular, contemporary, four-level restaurant with a boutique full of gifts, crafts and textiles that she purchases all over the Indonesian archipelago. She also owns *Murni's Houses*, an enclave of serene, rustic cottages on the hill in Ubud's Campuhan section.

On the afternoon before *Galungan*, Murni's father finishes the bamboo altar outside the wall that surrounds the family compound. Murni sits on her porch at home making offerings. Her life has revolved around business, but this year, 'I made a choice. I would take two weeks off to learn this art. It is time.' She and four women on her staff are putting the finishing touches on 200 holiday offerings, enough for all her enterprises and her house. Murni weaves leaves together, making a pedestal to contain fruit and flowers. She will begin her *Galungan* celebration at home. 'In the morning, we will pray in our temple, which includes an altar for Vishnu, the sun god, and altars to our ancestors,' she tells us.

Already, at Murni's family temple, her helpers are placing tier upon tier of offerings: apples, pink *jambu* fruit, eggs, cakes, cookies, meats carved into filigrees, layers of flowers, cones of rice, vegetables and spices. There are swags of the ubiquitous black-and-white checkered fabric. There are perfect pyramids of fruit. Surely, we think, the ancestors will be delighted.

Paola Gianturco is a photojournalist and author whose first book, *In Her Hands: Craftswomen Changing the World* was co-authored with Toby Tuttle (Monacelli Press/NYC, 2000) and included a chapter about women artisans in Ubud who create beautiful handmade offerings. Photograph by Marge d'Wylde.

Labour and Love

Dr. Sylvia Tiwon

As a group of friends sat overlooking the water, the sun sank slowly into the horizon, touching Murni's face with a golden glow and brushing crimson into her hair. This was not Bali, however, but Berkeley, California, where Mary Letterii, Murni's close friend in San Francisco, had invited us to a get-together. Nor was Murni on vacation—of course not! She was here on a working trip and had spent the entire day preparing for two important trade shows. And yet, as she sat there in the setting sun, not a shred of fatigue lined her face and her warm good humour enveloped us all. I had only just come away from work and felt the detritus of the day in my limbs but her gentle jokes and spontaneous laughter soon dissolved all that and made me appreciate just how much of a tonic effect a deeply happy person could have: much better than happy hour at the bar.

Though I had known Murni in person for only a couple of years, I had heard about her as long ago as the 1970's, when university students and researchers would return to California from Indonesia and regale me with stories about Murni's little *warung* in Ubud where they had found good food, comfort and friendship: respite from some of the inevitable wear and tear of study abroad. Everyone knows that the little *warung*, nestled in the bend of Ubud's main road, has grown into a major enterprise by dint of her hard work and engaging personality, and I believe it is this love of labour and of people that has made her the happy person she is. In this, she represents the overwhelming majority of Balinese women.

Not long after the first parliamentary elections following the fall of Soeharto's New Order, I was asked to assist in facilitating a newly formed parliamentary women's caucus. The series of meetings of newly elected women members of parliament was intended to identify the special needs of women and children that had been largely ignored during the previous era and had only come to the surface during the economic and political crises that had overwhelmed Indonesian society in 1998-99.

The meetings were attended by elected women representatives from all over Indonesia. As I opened the first session I was facilitating, I noticed a lone gentleman sitting somewhat awkwardly in the circle of women. Participants then took turns to say their name and the place they represented: Aceh, North Sumatra, South Sumatra, etc., through the island of Java, and then came the turn of the male MP. 'I represent Bali,' he said. He must have noticed the looks of surprise—if not outright amazement—from all the women around him, for he continued, 'I have come to Jakarta to represent Balinese women because they are all too hard at work to come here to represent themselves.' In the days and eventually years that followed, I came to better understand and appreciate the deeply complex nature of the work that women did in homes, in temples, in the arts and crafts and in the local and global marketplace. Today, Bali also has women representatives in parliament. But to me—and I know to many others—Murni is the ultimate embodiment of a serene elegance which marks her labour as love.

Dr. Sylvia Tiwon teaches the literatures and cultures of Indonesia at the University of California in Berkeley. A graduate of the University of Indonesia, she continued her graduate education in California. Her publications include *Breaking the Spell: Colonialism and Literary Renaissance in Indonesia*, as well as articles on culture, politics and women. She also loves to cook and is a firm believer in the benefits of shared meals.

In Dire Need of a Cold Drink, Cookies and Fried Bananas

Mary Letterii

The first time I saw Murni she was standing behind the bamboo bar at *Murni's Warung* laughing. She was in conversation with her husband Pat who was seated at the bar facing her wearing a navy blue T-shirt which spelled out in large white letters, 'Mr Murni'. It was a blisteringly hot late afternoon in June 1976, one of those rare days with nary a breeze when all of Ubud seemed to move in slow motion. I walked in with my boyfriend Curt and our friend Ian—the three of us woozy from the heat and in dire need of a cold drink.

On a bus trip back to Bali from Yogyakarta a day earlier, Ian had regaled us with stories of *Murni's Warung*, as far as he was concerned, the best place to eat in all of Bali. And in his much appreciated role as our old Bali-hand benefactor he promised to take us there, just as he had led us to so many other wonderful places in the three weeks we'd known each other. As we rode along through small towns and villages in East Java, I thought about the enchanting restaurant Ian described, lit by antique kerosene lamps and situated at the very end of the village, right before the bridge that connects Ubud to Campuhan. I noted the warmth with which he spoke about Murni and her husband Pat, a former Peace Corp volunteer in Afghanistan and a writer, Ian told us, who left the United States in 1968 and whose dry sense of humor was a fine match to his own ever-present sense of the absurd.

'Good day, Mr Caldwell,' Pat greeted Ian in a relaxed soft voice with a put-on British accent as he pulled out three bar stools while Murni extended her hand from behind the bar and introduced herself. 'Please have something cold to drink,' she said, offering us three frosted beer mugs from a beautiful old Coca-Cola cooler. Within minutes, we were all sitting together at the bar happily talking, me and Ian and Curt with our ice-cold beer Bintangs. I was in that revved-up happy state of expectation you feel knowing that great new friends have just entered your life.

Living in Peliatan that summer and autumn, we ate at *Murni's Warung* every night we weren't in a far-off part of Bali or traveling in Java. *Murni's Warung* was our base, our home, and Pat and Murni became our family. In those early days of the *Warung* the first few items on the menu were a sampling of simple, expertly prepared Indonesian recipes—to this day I've never had better *saté ayam, nasi goreng* or black rice pudding—and the sort of fresh, familiar and similarly well-prepared Western food many travelers craved but couldn't easily find—hamburgers, guacamole, homemade yogurt, chocolate cake and pie. I saw Murni's curiosity in action right away—she wanted to excel, and to that end she quizzed guests about her food—did they like it? How could it be improved? Would they prepare it differently? 'We're learning as we go along,' she'd say modestly. Not once did I hear anyone offer a peep of a suggestion about the meal they'd just consumed with gusto but various friends did offer to teach Murni their own specialties. Many a convivial cooking session ensued in the *Warung's* kitchen during those months, with the most satisfactorily mastered dishes finding inclusion in the burgeoning menu and named after the friend who taught Murni the recipe. Sometimes Murni's twelve-year old son, Toko, joined us; he was a quiet boy with a sweet and helpful presence who seemed to enjoy being in the midst of that extroverted, bustling kitchen with its array of woks, ingredients, tantalizing aromas and non-stop flow of personalities.

As anyone who knows Murni can attest, she has a generous, intensely empathetic and compassionate nature. Her acute intuition and sensitivity is a gift borne of pain. When she was seven, her parents divorced, which was uncommon and stigmatizing. In an act of revenge against her mother, Murni's father exercised his right to separate mother and daughter. Murni was sent to live with her father's family in Campuhan and forbidden to speak with her mother. During one of our many long walks in Ubud, Murni showed me the place where she used to hide behind bushes on market day to catch a glimpse of her mother making her way to the *pasar*. Eventually she shored up enough nerve to call out to her mother, and the two of them began meeting there regularly until Murni was caught and harshly punished. After all these years, I haven't forgotten the image of Murni and her mother huddled behind those bushes, her mother offering her *nasi bungkus* [rice and bits of spiced chicken or beef wrapped in a banana leaf] and cake and for a few powerful moments showering her with affection before both had to return to work.

Murni worked as hard as a child could, climbing coconut trees every morning to gather firewood, ironing clothes for her father's family and in early morning hours preparing sticky rice, cookies and fried bananas to sell with coffee and tea. Those were just a few of her tasks. Her early morning labor caused her to be late for school every day, which embarrassed her. But she was buoyed by her teacher, a sympathetic soul who understood her situation, always made her welcome and to her eternal gratitude spared her the embarrassment of a public reprimand.

Dazzled by the spectacular beauty of Bali, the immense warmth and creativity of the Balinese, and immediately at ease in a culture where my natural friendliness was responded to in kind, Murni became my closest friend, my confidante and my guide. On our walks she showed me special, out-of-the-way places. She listened with infinite patience to my endless questions about ceremonies, food, offerings and domestic life and was unstinting and brave in her answers.

Murni's gifted character is now legendary and her exquisite taste, collection of rare textiles and antiques are well documented, but her greatest gift and the open secret to her success is her gift for friendship. I love her dearly.

Mary Letterii grew up in an Irish-Italian family in Poughkeepsie, New York and moved to San Francisco in 1975, where she attended San Francisco State University and graduated with a BA in English and Creative Writing. She has worked as a secretary, an ESL instructor, and a photo researcher. In the early 1980's she was part of a team that provided social services to Vietnamese, Cambodian and Laotian refugees at the Center for Southeast Asian Refugee Resettlement in San Francisco's Tenderloin neighborhood, where she discovered the wonders of *khao pun, larb gai* and *banh mi*. Mary has been working on a documentary film about an Indonesian poet and former political prisoner for many years and has made her living as a biotech recruiter since the 1990's.

Where's My Doggy Bag?

Dausa

Dr. Lawrence Blair was first researching his documentary *Bali—Island of the Dogs* and stopped by for a cold drink with his friend. I was sleeping in the sun on the steps of my mistress's restaurant and the two of them startled me—Blair with his eye patch and Jagger with those big lips. And I say to myself, 'So what if I growl at them!' And anyway, I was more worried that Sir Mick might actually bite me. But I don't want to make a special case of Messieurs Blair and Jagger—because in Ubud any and every human who visited my mistress's *Warung* walked over me—or should I say—had to walk over me.

Yes, I was a 'watch dog'—as is the chief characteristic of my breed (Balinese people believe that some of us can see ghosts and so like us around to keep bad spirits away from their homes—and maybe I could) but I grew fat and very content on that front step. There were so many great treats and so little time. Sometimes guests would order especially for me and have 'saté for Dausa' added to their bill. The truth is, I deserved every morsel—especially Murni's chocolate chip cookies. I was a Kintamani dog in that life—a close cousin to the Australian Dingo—but far, far more cultured. (We would never eat a baby.)

Indigenous to the Kintamani region, experts on animal genetics have pointed out that my breed has the richest pool of genetic diversity in all of dogdom, and can trace our ancestry right back to the proto-dogs, whereas all other mere 'breeds' are barely a couple of centuries old. According to the Balinese *Pawukon* calendar, I was auspiciously born on the one-day week of *Ekawara-Luang* in the mountain village of Dausa— and so I was named.

I was given to Ibu Murni in the same year her *Warung* first opened—1974, by a kindly old man. As a pup, I was brown with a black chest—a colour the Balinese humans call *belang bungkem*—the perfect colour and age to be sacrificed at a purification ceremony—but, thanks to the kindness of my mistress, I was to enjoy another destiny—head guard dog to *Murni's Warung*.

A pious Kintamani dog, like a pious Balinese, leads a busy and crowded life full of rites and ceremonies, whose purpose is to cleanse the unclean, reconcile the irreconcilable, worship, appease, avert danger, obtain nourishment and secure a happy life after death and a good reincarnation. I was buried with two chocolate chip cookies made by Ibu Murni's son Toko on a plot of land at *Murni's Houses*, which is right behind where Ibu Murni has built a beautiful *balé*.

Was I reincarnated? Perhaps I was. Or perhaps my spirit still resides on the sunny front step of the most famous *Warung* in all of Bali. And if you are curious—like many humans are— just leave a tasty *saté* stick out and see how long it lasts.

But I have jumped too far ahead of myself. After 40 delicious courses, dessert is the culinary finale at *Murni's Warung*. And just too bad for everyone else—I'm going to order first. (There has to be some advantage to reincarnation.) I'd like a Dausa-sized piece of Murni's pecan pie and two—no, three—scoops of vanilla ice cream. And give me the menu. I'll eat that too!

Dausa was born in the village of Dausa in the highlands of Central Bali in 1974—he was a Kintamani dog in his last life, a connoisseur of many delicacies. Foremost amongst his species, Dausa dedicated his long and happy life to not moving far from the front step of *Murni's Warung*—and in doing so, he averted many dangers, obtained constant nourishment and secured a happy life after death and a good reincarnation. Photograph by Jonathan Copeland.

The Dessert Menu

Due to one of the contributors, the dessert menu is being redrafted and will appear in the second edition.